RUN KIWI RUN
BY RICHARD STEWART

Copyright 2021 Richard Stewart

Published by Flyover Books

All rights reserved.
No part of this book may be used or reproduced
in any manner whatsoever without written consent
from the publisher, except for brief quotations for reviews.

If you have questions about this book, you can reach the author at
richardstewartenterprises@outlook.com

FIRST EDITION
10 9 8 7 6 5 4 3 2 1
ISBN: 978-0-6451989-0-4

*To all my friends and family
who have had an impact on my life.*

This is a story about courage, about faith, about stepping out into the unknown, about trying to make sense of a world that is rapidly changing in views, morals and standards.

Most important is seeking God's will for my life in the struggles of growing up and into an adult, taking responsibilities for my actions, treating people fairly, helping the unloved and the downcast, whilst enjoying life's journey with the adventures along the way.

For any person reading this story, I hope you will be inspired by the motivation and the sacrifices to achieve goals and will not overlook people on your journey who have had misfortunes in life and need a gentle hand, either physically or mentally, or just need somebody there to listen.

If it wasn't for some of these people, I think my journey through life would have been a little different.

Important to note, laughter is a medicine. (*"A merry heart doth good like a medicine,"* said King Solomon in the book of Proverbs in the Bible). Laugh at yourself and make others laugh.

I would also like to thank my Mum and my Dad (Dad who has just recently passed away in the last two years) for the love and support they gave me growing up with my older brother and four sisters.

If it wasn't for their values and Christian teaching, which I hold onto again, my journey would have been a little different.

I have many friends who have worked with me and inspired me over the years, but in recent times, one in particular has asked me to write this book.

"Courage is what it takes to stand up for what's right and courage is also what it takes to sit down and listen."

This is my story.

Richard Stewart

The Early Years

During my early childhood years, I often got into trouble and extended my mum's boundaries. My dad, like me, had a sense of humor and saw the funny side to most things I did but he could be stern and non-compromising.

My mum was an English nurse who came to Australia to do her out training in Melbourne and worked as a bush nurse at Broken Hill, a famous mining town in NSW.

My father met my mum on a ship as he was travelling on a ship from New Zealand to an international Scout Jamboree in England and Mum was travelling home to Yorkshire.

Dad travelled back to the United Kingdom, working in Europe and traveling on his motorbike where Mum was. Eventually they got married in England 1960 and came to live on the east coast of the North Island of New Zealand, a place called Gisborne, a place where Captain James Cook left his mark.

Dad was a building contractor and would often take my brother and me to work with him on our holidays and some Saturdays. Dad mainly built houses, farm sheds, and some commercial buildings, eventually building his own commercial properties.

I remember Dad had a flat deck old Bedford truck with an old push start ignition. As a five-year-old, I would play in the truck, which happened to be down by the riverside this day. The truck had been left in gear and I had somehow managed to start it, the truck began moving and it was great just steering it till I saw my Dad in a panic, running after his truck and me in it.

Well, that moment didn't go down too well for either of us.

There were times my brother and I would help stack precut timber for house frames for Dad and one day Dad stacked and removed timber from his trailer, ensuring we were both off. I decided to climb onto the trailer without him noticing and sat there quietly whilst he drove away.

It wasn't till he got down the street a bit he saw me through his mirror sitting on the trailer and to his shock immediately stopped and grabbed me, taking me straight home.

The things I put my dear mother through. My mother was a great knitter. She knitted all our woolen clothing. There was one time she had been knitting me this jersey by the fire. It was nearly complete. She went out of the room, wondering what she would do if I threw it in the fire (which I did). Well, I saw the other side of her wooden spoon.

These were just some of the things I got up to in a time where families cared and interacted with each other in the 1960s, 1970s, and early 1980s.

We made things out of nothing growing up and had fun doing it. We made go-carts, pushing them down hills, sometimes falling off, sometimes scratching ourselves or bleeding a little. Building tree huts to watch the boat races out in the bay, building sand bunkers to play war games. Swimming, fishing, participating in the Scouts, camping, having the courage to create and invent stupid things.

THE EARLY YEARS

We got into trouble once firing sky rockets next door on Guy Fawkes night, which was probably a dumb thing to do.

We lived across the road from the beach in Gisborne, so part of the beach was for swimming and down further was for surfers. In the 1970s, we had professional surfing bum houses at the end of the street. Although they might have been on the benefit (dole), they made the best of surfing every day. (My brother and I did surf. Andrew was more into it than me.)

Each end of the beach had surf lifesaving clubs and this one fella from the midway surf club used to ride his motor scooter up and down our street. He just seemed so annoying. Even more funny, he wore this bowl helmet with leather side straps (completely old style).

Well, my brother and I waited for him to ride his usual ride into the sunset and as he passed, we threw a handful of stones at him and ran back down the driveway. No joking, he turned around and drove down our driveway and abruptly gave Mother a message on how to control her boys.

My brother and I were around the corner laughing our heads off until Mother came out with wooden spoons, which had some effect on tender bums.

Dad had proudly built the family home. A two-storied five-bedroom house with a two-car basement. He turned the old

establishment in the front where we originally lived into units.

One of these units became my English grandparents' home when they retired and came out to live in the sunny shores of New Zealand. My mother was an only child and my grandparents reluctantly came out from England to be with family and we were always reminded how things were better back in Yorkshire. (Yorkshire today is full of foreign nationals, sorry, Grandpa.)

Our family were swimmers involved in swimming clubs. I was actually the school swimming champion at primary school one year, receiving a trophy at the end of that year. Don't know how that happened.

We were all in other sports as well, my brother and me in Rugby Union and Cricket and my two sisters in netball. Being involved in the Salvation Army church, we all learnt to play brass and my parents worked to be able to afford for us to play piano.

My brother and I were interested in other activities and I have to say my sisters became more proficient at playing piano than my brother or me.

Later on, I will tell you about band trips I was involved in nationally and internationally.

When looking back over our high school years, Dad had an active role in Scouts as he held a Queen Scouts award and his ability to organise and take our scout troop on hikes through bushland, lakes, to jamborees, and his assistant was in the Speleologist Society and he was actively able to get us involved in caving and climbing underground. We would be crawling underground at times, down waterfalls, and chimney our way back up through the cracks to the top surface.

Dad also rebuilt a boat to take the Scouts waterskiing. Dad was just adventurous. (I think that is where I got it from.)

THE EARLY YEARS

However my brother and I received Chief Scouts awards and I went on to complete my Duke of Edinburgh Gold award. This was presented to me at Government House by the then Governor General, the late Sir Keith Holyoak, in November 1979 on behalf of Prince Phillip.

My parents were loving Christian people who taught us to love one another as Christ loved us, to love our neighbour's (which can be over a broad spectrum), and to encourage people, doing it all for Christ.

My mother grew up in the dark days of WW2 in Britain. As an only child, she knew what it was to live on a knife's edge with the enemy at the door, rations, bomb shelters and destruction and death all around. Mum used to tell me how her parents billeted soldiers who had been evacuated from the beaches of Dunkirk, France at the start of the German invasion of France. But with courage, spirit and conviction to never give up and good leadership of the British people, history was changed and the British Isles maintained their sovereignty (with the help of the colonials and the USA).

My mother is eighty-six years old now and I can still remember her as my young nursing mother, supporting and caring for all our family.

My father travelled overseas fifteen years after WW2 through Europe, initially beginning with an international Scout jamboree in England (I think he said he had met Lord Bayden Powell, the man who established the Scouting movement over in England) and then working and motorbike riding through Europe before meeting my mother. (I used to have Dad's old WW2 RAF flying jacket which was double wooled lined leather jacket before it got stolen when my house got broken into some years ago). My father passed away two years ago (Oct 2017) unexpectedly but I will tell you a big story about my father and my episodes later.

THE EARLY YEARS

Our family grew up in a time where we were encouraged to think outside the square to achieve.

To earn money for projects, we mowed lawns, delivered papers, bought and sold bikes, pulled down old chimneys, cleaned up the bricks and sold them, and painted houses.

My father and brother also rebuilt and painted cars. They were very good at that as well. We were involved in youth groups and youth group activities.

Two funny things come to mind with Scout camps. We were out on a camp one weekend out in the bush and a few of us must have disturbed a Tasmanian wasp nest. These things just keep stinging. They were in our shirts and up our shirts and the closest thing to relieve the pain was running, stripping off, and jumping into the river.

The second funniest thing I can remember is trying to smoke tea leaves wrapped up in toilet paper. Don't recommend it. (Brother's idea.) It was similar experience trying a cigar. You don't inhale, as I found out very quickly. I have never smoked or wanted to after that, having seen my English grandfather suffer emphysema from smoking.

Christmas and school holidays were great. Every second year, we would camp with our cousins down the South Island of New Zealand on beaches, fishing expeditions, hiking through the wilderness of central Otago. And every other year we would be camping or boating as a family somewhere in the North Island of New Zealand at or near the beaches as a family.

I remember one of the funniest times when we were camping up at the Bay of Islands. We arrived and all the camping grounds were filled with holiday-makers. The best site of all had a "no camping" sign pegged out. Didn't take long to realise the "no camping" sign would come in handy for a tent pole. A little while later more people came and camped beside us and not long after that, the boys in blue came down asking if we had seen that "no camping" sign. (What "No Camping" sign?)

Dad had refurbished a boat and was always improving it, strengthening the hull with fibre glass and finding a bigger motor on board. I never ever saw my mom or dad arguing about money for holidays. They just made it happen. Dad was a master at refurbishing things. We even used this boat, taking the Scouts water skiing on the river as well as fishing trips later on.

But there were times not so good for Dad. Dad would have to deal with difficult people in business and privately and sometimes I think he was taken advantage of for his goodness. For example, he

THE EARLY YEARS

would house people in his rentals who had lost the accommodation or he would not be completely paid for building contracts he had completed. Still, he would take groceries to people who had lost their jobs. Sometimes having to spend the extra hours away from home to ensure all our needs were met and have a roof over our head. (This had an effect on some of my siblings, which I will cover later).

I sometimes feel I inherited a little of these traits, which happened later to me in business but later built up a strong discernment with who to deal with and not to deal with.

Growing up with pets, dogs were a good challenge mainly for me and my mother. The best dog we ever had was a German Shepard named Kaiser. Mum and I would look after him and take him for runs. I even pulled him away from a scrape one day with an unmuzzled Greyhound on the beach.

The Greyhound went for me and got bitten. The owner took off with his dog quickly and I still have the scars from teeth marks in my leg to this day, which had to be stitched. Kaiser was unhurt.

Some nights, he would come and sleep on my bed when I was living at home and he stood as tall as me when on his hind legs playing with me. Kaiser was also a very protective dog. Kaiser did however manage to break his front leg one day and his recovery was a little slow as he was always trying to take the plaster and bandages off but he did heal.

Eventually, Kaiser developed the sickness which shepherds get in their back legs and kidney functions. Kaiser had to be put down.

We did have a beautiful portrait of him, which my parents kept for many years.

One of the tragedies when I think back is I didn't have a pet for my two lovely girls growing up, thinking a pet would never be looked after as my own siblings never had much to do in looking after Kaiser, just Mother and me. (This was a bit selfish on my behalf.)

Anyways, high school came and went. I was involved in Rugby Union (with the school and Club Rugby against the school where I got knocked out deliberately), Cricket, Air Cadets where I learnt to fly (De Havilland Tiger Moth Biplane) and fire a rifle. Later I bought the Biplane. That's another story.

But with rugby, I was that good at my position as No. 8 and Flanker someone took offense to me. I got knocked out and landed up in hospital with concussion. It was the last game I played.

Growing into an Adult

High school in 1976 started to change how I wanted to aim professionally when leaving school.

I had to work real hard as I was not an academic, but I found that I could still achieve good grades if I worked hard. (Still have my old school reports and results).

My teachers wanted their students to learn well and they had a good input to all the lives of students who wanted to learn and some even would take the time with those who were a little disadvantaged to keep up with other students.

Quite a few of these teachers were ex-servicemen from WW2 and the Korean conflict.

Geoff Sharp, my English teacher and principal, was a squadron leader in the battle of Britain.

Campbell Prentice, my economics teacher and family friend, flew the Famous Mosquitos in the Pathfinders squadron over Europe for the RNZAF.

The deputy principal was a Navy officer in the RNZN on the New Zealand ship Ajax and with the British Navy ambushed and sank the German battleship in the Graf Spee in the Battle of the River Plate South America.

My engineering teacher flew on Lockheed Hudson Twin engine bombers in the Pacific Theatre up until 1945, I believe. (Still kept in contact with him many years after I had left school.)

Makes me feel old and you can probably guess what vintage I am.

Getting back to school, these were teachers who loved to teach and see great results in their students and these men and woman gave me incentives, ideals, and dreams to aim for.

They taught accountability, responsibility and to never quit when the going got tough.

At the end of 1977, during my second year at high school, my family had a Christmas in Australia.

We hired a Volkswagen Kombi van fully equipped with awning and a pop up roof for accommodation, sleeping all six of us, including Mum and Dad.

We landed in Brisbane, drove to Sydney and Melbourne (places we stopped were Old Sydney Town, Bathurst, and rural areas of northern NSW) then onto Adelaide and back around the outer parts of NSW, Port Macquarie, and also visiting friends in two states. And from there we went to southern NSW then flew out from Sydney back to New Zealand. A three week holiday in all.

For me, visiting made-up castles, aviation museums, camping in rural areas, seeing friends, moving around cities, and beach hopping was one of the best family holidays we had together.

1976-1977 prepared me for senior high school.

The following year was Form Five and in New Zealand was school certificate year. (First national exams sat every year). I was very uneasy with exams although I had sat and passed many over the years preceding.

Some people are creative in building and designing, which was me all over and some people are good at exams with little effort, which wasn't me.

I stayed at school for another two years. The subjects completed were maths (wonderful maths teacher who later died at an early age from Parkinson's Disease), Physics, Engineering, Tech Drawing. In those last two years, it brought the end of my rugby engagements as I landed in hospital with a concussion.

But in those two years before leaving school, I bought and sold anything I could lay my hands on to raise money to start learning to fly light aircraft. Before leaving school in 1980, I did my first solo in ZK DNJ registration of aircraft at Gisborne airport.

Yep, flew my first solo! The instructor got out of plane and said, "You are on your own," closed the hatch and walked back to the aeroclub. It was a great feeling.

It was another few months after I had completed my 6th form year in 1980 that I contemplated what I would do to complete the hours and exams and finally the flight test for a private pilot license and what job would I need to support flying activities.

You will see how crazy I had become to support my passion in flying.

I was turned down by the New Zealand Air Force as I started to wear glasses for distance as a pilot for flight crew.

Then I was told by the New Zealand Civil Aviation Authority that they would not grant me a class 1 medical as I wore glasses. (Class one for commercial pilots, that's what I was aiming for.)

My father gave me work for a short period and, through his contacts, I was accepted as the last electrical apprentice for the 1981 year intake. This was with the local power supply authority on the east coast area of the North Island of New Zealand.

I would like to thank the Rasmussen family whose father was my engineering boss. The chief engineer interviewed me for that position and gave me the apprenticeship. With my background in Scouts, music achievements, and being awarded a Duke of Edinburgh Gold at Government House, plus the hard effort and achievements I made at school, he believed he could offer me this apprenticeship as an electrician.

It was the only five years that I worked for anyone this long in my electrical working history.

This was my income. I had affordable accommodation at home. This would help me finish off the cost to achieving my private pilot license.

By August 1981, the RNZAF (Air Force) had accepted me for the

THE EARLY YEARS

engineering program, but I turned it down as having been eight months into my electrical apprenticeship.

During that time also the New Zealand Civil Aviation Authority had changed its requirements for pilots who wore glasses and I was able to meet the class 1 medical requirements. (This was due to a number of existing commercial pilots who were having to wear glasses in later years.)

All of 1981, I would flight train about three times a week. I would save a good portion of my salary for this. (From the early 1980s, I can remember paying $30 p/h and progressively the cost rose to about $60 p/h). I would subsidise my training with buying and selling, rebuilding pushbikes, mowing lawns, and cleaning up bricks from old chimneys which were pulled down.

My income as an apprentice was $120 per week the first year. This is how focused you needed to be.

Some days my work would be out of town, other days I would have work in town. When work was in town at the electrical switchyards, I would go flying in my lunch break. (Remember I had an hour for lunch and would jump on a push bike and race to the airport and train for a half hour). When looking back, I am not sure how I managed to do this but it happened.

One thing I will mention: God deserves all the glory for the life, family, and friends he continues to give me.

In-between my flight training and sitting aviation exams, I was also studying for trade exams. My sister was studying to become a nurse and another sister was going through teacher's college. My older brother had finished or had nearly finished his building apprenticeship with my dad's business.

Working with the supply authority actually gave me time to study when work was a bit slack. The smoko room was a good quiet place to get into theory books.

Working with the east coast power board was enjoyable. I worked on and rebuilt transformers, worked and maintained electrical substations and tested heavy electrical equipment in the testing department. These tradesmen I worked with taught me so much, which helped me in later years in the heavy industrial fixed plant and mobile plant maintenance.

The other passion in my life was music. I played my cornet in the Salvation Army bands and later in orchestras, doing trumpet concertos and going on band tours with the Salvation Army.

As you can see, my life was full, not to say I didn't have challenges and disappointments. I failed my trade exam once and my aviation exams twice, but this didn't mean I was any the less capable of both of these. It just made me work harder.

My first cross country flight was done in May 1981 within 200 nautical miles. The first was from Gisborne to Hastings via Napier on the east coast and the second was from Gisborne to Rotorua (North Island). I think the first trip Dad came and I was under instruction with an instructor both trips. There is a lot of planning that goes into these flights and in the more advance training to instrument flight rules, the flying precision is even greater.

The third cross country was my solo cross country. Navigating my way VFR (visual flight rules) from Gisborne to Rotorua and back with having had good map training. This flight was flown across Lake Rotoma, Lake Rotoiti, and Rotorua Airport is situated alongside Lake Rotorua. I returned back to Gisborne the same way as I had come only in the reverse direction.

Most of my work friends were out partying or telling how they got drunk on the weekends. There were sometimes I had to cover as a sober driver for them.

My goal was to finish my private pilot license training and enjoy the company of my group of friends having real fun.

It was during this time in early 1981 that I met another young Christian man who was training as an air traffic controller in Gisborne. It was weird he was a Kiwi with an American accent. (His parents had been missionaries in Japan in the 1950s from the call of General Douglas MacArthur as one of many admired families who went to work and live with Japanese people after the second

THE EARLY YEARS   15

world war.)

Dave went to an American Air Force base school in Japan only to come back to finish his high school education in Wellington, New Zealand and here he was. I will call him Dave for the purpose of this book. We became good friends and quite often he would come over for dinner. (Mum would always have a spare plate at the table). Dave would come to youth groups and I think he even may have come camping at one stage as well.

Well, through Dave I got to know most of the air traffic controllers in the area and did we have some fun. Some of them even came to social soccer games and other sporting activities.

Now let me tell you, we did some things at the airport that were extremely fun. The main runway at the Gisborne Airport is Runway 14, magnetic at one end, and 32 in the opposite direction. The runway has a set of train lines running through the runway, so of course if a train is coming and an aircraft is about to land to take off, the train is in contact with the control tower and has to stop and give to aircraft. (There are only two train lines running through airports in the Southern hemisphere and Gisborne is one of them).

Now at times, especially late on weekends, flights in and out of the airport were low. (Training aircraft could use the other grass runways.) We would race our super sports cars, a bit like top gear but 1980s style and no Jeremy Clarkson or James May.

Most aircraft today have radios which are VHF, HF for communication and nav aids. (Advance technology has brought GPS and glass cockpit configuration). Years ago there were some aircraft (mainly vintage aircraft) to take off and land. They were given a series of lights:
- Green or flashing green for go.
- Red or flashing red for stop or danger, be on the alert.
- White for caution.

Today pilots still have to know the colors for in case of radio loss (professional pilots cannot be color blind).

Going back to the races, from the tower Dave would flash a

green light for go and a red light for stop. Our racing cars were the infamous Triumph Stag, the old GT Ford Capri, and of course the Datsun GT Special and a few others. 1500 meters or more allowed us to clock up some speed.

Now I am talking about some years ago. Today this would be something terrible to the politically correct people who make our laws. However, we made our fun and growing up in these years were sometimes difficult but as friends we relied on each other.

Dave was in town for almost five years before being transferred to another secondary unit and then to a major unit on radar in Wellington, New Zealand. I did rent with Dave in later years, as I will mention in the story.

I gained my private pilot license at the end of 1981, my first big achievement completed at the age of nineteen. (It would take me another five years to complete my commercial pilot license.)

In the four years from 1981 till June 1985, my electrical apprenticeship was completed. My trade certificate was passed with very high marks.

There is another twist to the story as in those first two years of my apprenticeship and living at home, I met up with another fella. He was in the Canadian Navy and his ship had pulled into the port of Gisborne having escorted the Queens Britannia for the 1982 Commonwealth Games in Brisbane.

Daniel came along to a special weekend we were having at the Salvation Army Church in Gisborne. We had a visiting band and a big picnic at the domain. Daniel brought along one of his French Canadian officers and having had a great time that weekend in return wanted to take a few of us all over his ship (not allowed to the public). We went down to the engine room. He showed us the desalination plant converting salt water into fresh drinking water, the accommodation, onto the bridge, and a quick look at the armament. That was Sunday till midnight.

From that time on, I kept in contact with Daniel for the next few years.

The Next Adventure was Starting to Unfold.

June 1985, having completed my apprenticeship, I passed everything and gained my electrical license. I had saved enough money to haul a backpacking expedition overseas and took a trip to Europe, the USA and Canada to eventually catch up with Daniel.

I resigned from the Power Supply Authority. I am not sure if they were happy to see me leave or sad. What I did learn from the last department I was in, which was the electrical inspectors, would stay entrenched in my electrical career down the track.

Sad to note that when the government deregulated and removed the supply authorities, the electrical standards dropped. You cannot beat experience and knowledge. This disappointing effect has had repercussions not only in the electrical industry but in other industries as well, with politicians having made laws with no clues about how it will affect these high performing industries.

Overseas Adventure 1985.

During the years of my apprenticeship, living at home with cheap rent gave me a chance to save for an overseas adventure. Keeping the grounds tidy and keeping the inside of my parents' place clean and paying a board allowance helped me to save. Mum and Dad gave me and all my brothers a head start in life, showing us how to sacrifice for long term gain.

I left New Zealand at the age of twenty-four and headed to the Netherlands where I had a family friend who worked as a manager for Mobil Oil in The Haag or Den Haag, as the Dutch call it. They would be away for the first few weeks when arriving in the Netherlands and I would see them later.

My flight route was from Auckland, New Zealand to Singapore

to India (New Delhi) to Amsterdam. I knew no one, just had blind faith and my backpack.

This is Amsterdam in the summer: lots of people, lots of tourists, lots of lovely young ladies, lots of helpful people.

On the flight over, I cannot forget sitting next to a Canadian family who were travelling around the world for a couple of days. This was funny but they didn't think so. All the money they had spent for just a few days and here I was having travelled thirty-six hours and jet-lagged.

As I moved on, my back pack slung over my shoulders, an American fella came up to me and asked me if I needed accommodation. I said yes, not realizing till later that the more clients he got to stay on this river boat in the canal, the more free nights he got. It wasn't such a bad deal because breakfast was included. The man running the show was a German named Sehrnetter Mann, a very nice man.

It was good to stay for a few nights and see the city of Amsterdam in the summer, barrel organs rumbling in the square, lots of musicians, markets, boats moving in the canals, Dutch markets, museums and many other attractions. It was a time you could change world currencies at the bank before euros became the European currency. So New Zealand dollars for Dutch Guilders was a good deal as it was one of the only countries in Europe that the New Zealand dollar traded higher. The German Deutschmark was a lot stronger at the time, as I later found out.

Amsterdam was great. As I moved around the city, I was able to see other historical artifacts, the ports, and how the Dutch lived.

I moved on to Rotterdam to meet up with Darrel and Laura from New Zealand. They were pleased to see me, having initially rocked up to Darrel's company office (Mobile Oil in The Netherlands) with my backpack. His lovely secretary sat me down with a cup of coffee and, seeing how tired I looked, offered me some sympathy. I lapped it all up. She was very nice. The office itself was in the Haag or Den Haag (outside Rotterdam) as the Dutch pronounce it. This is where the international law courts and war crimes tribunals are, as well as where international banking between countries on a big scale is done.

Darrell and Laura had a company house and it was very nice to sleep in a bed again, enjoy some good food, good company, and a good swim in their pool. They appreciated the time, since they were so far away from family and New Zealand.

Darrell and Laura drove me through on the weekends to the open markets where you could buy almost anything from household to fruits, veg, clothes, cooked food, anything (not talking about illegal items although marijuana was legal to buy).

Darrell had the urge to take me somewhere that would broaden my education. I did not know what he meant at first till he drove me down to the Red Light district of Rotterdam. I was a little stunned seeing woman in windows, not just woman but pretty women waving at you, enticing you to come and play with them at a price. Turning to Darrel, I said, "I'm not paying, let's go." He just laughed. Couldn't believe he had taken me there.

The cities of Amsterdam and Rotterdam are renowned for Red Light districts and marijuana clubs. But having said that, Darrell and Laura did take me to places that were historical and that had been bombed out and rebuilt after the Second World War. One of the places was called Delft. I have a photo of me walking around Delft in clogs.

Darrell and Laura had some pets they had brought with them after Darrell had been transferred from Mobil Oil Zambia to Mobil Oil the Netherlands. They had a Bullmastiff dog and two Siamese cats. This Bullmastiff with a ridge back and strong legs was gentle as anything and it would take some effort to make it aggressive. You wouldn't want to do that anyways. (Later when these pets were taken back to New Zealand and placed in quarantine, they did become very aggressive when released. Their nature changed after confinement).

After having stayed for a few days, it was time to utilise a push bike and I decided to go across country on the cobble bicycle tracks.

I was in Rotterdam one day. In the Netherlands, bicycles have the right of way over cars and jaywalking (crossing the road anywhere at any angle) is illegal. We do it all the time at our own risk but not in this part of the world. However, not knowing this, I jaywalked one day in front of a police van. All of a sudden, the van cut me off across the foot path and a police officer asked what I was doing in a thick Dutch accent. Immediately I replied, pretending I didn't understand. They advised me if I made a road crossing like that again, the station would be happy to accommodate me to help with their enquiries.

I realised riding a bike in the Netherlands had some advantages until you got a flat tyre.

So I borrowed Darrell's pushbike. In the Netherlands, everything is flat and also sinking. In Amsterdam itself, they were always repairing cobble streets because parts were sinking. As a flat country, many cross country tracks for push bikes had been constructed and I decided to carry on my adventure, riding a bicycle with a lighter backpack for a few days.

Flat tyres don't go down too well on cobblestone highways. Fixed and back on the road, I made my way to a very popular beach on the North Sea coast called Scheveningen. When the Dutch pronounce words, it sounds like they got something stuck in their throat or they're about to cough up phlegm from their throat. The name scheveningen could not be pronounced by Germans during the Second World War and many German spies were caught out because of this.

I didn't think much of the beaches on the North Sea as it looked

THE NEXT ADVENTURE WAS STARTING TO UNFOLD

dirty compared to the clean surfing beaches of New Zealand. Also many people would completely strip off here to lap up the sun in the summer months and fold up shops were everywhere along the beach during this time of year but packed up during the cold winter months.

Continuing riding, I passed windmills (the Dutch call them Mollens), saw famous dykes, stayed in youth hostels, and dressed in Dutch clothing and wore their clogs. It was great. There is also a Queen of the Netherlands; she was riding in her horse and carriage for some military display like the Queen of England and the trooping of the colors.

Eventually I dropped the bike off at Darrell's place, having ridden a few kilometers, and used my train ticket around Europe.

I said my goodbyes to Darrell and Laura and thanked them for a great stay. There was a possibility they were going home to New Zealand and would be there before I returned.

Travelling around Europe on a train pass was great. I bought a ticket for unlimited travel anywhere in Europe for a period of time. The only confusing part when rocking up to a city was the stations were situated North, South, East, West, in and from the same city. This was back in the late 1980s and early 1990s.

There was this one time I was coming back to Amsterdam late one night on a train and there was just a few of us, no accommodation open. Not even sure why I was on this train but there happened to be this American girl all by herself. She was unsure what to do. We stayed together all night in the park just talking till the morning. Her name was Hollie and she was meeting up with friends sometime the next day. Hollie was from Chicago. She was a young hotel manager on vacation here. It was cold that night and my heavy jersey became her jersey for the night. (I wrapped her up in it). That night she told me she had travelled to meet up with friends and hadn't realised not every hotel was open late at night to receive guests. We talked about places in Europe to see, how much she could pack into a few weeks in this part of the world. We talked about her family, what she was wanting to do in the future, where her friends were going to be. Hollie asked me what I was doing here and was thankful that I could be there with her at this time in European city she didn't know. We talked till dawn.

After seeing the morning sunrise and a few shops starting to open, Hollie felt OK to move on. She gave me a big hug and we went our separate ways. I did speak to her once more but we never saw each other again.

From leaving Darrell and Laura's place and leaving Hollie, the German border was not far away. My next training was towards the Southern parts of West Germany (Deutschland). In these times, there were border guards with semiautomatic guns checking passports as it is unfortunately today with terrorists in this part of the world. The guards were checking passports and identification. It was a time many Aussies and Kiwis travelled together and another time I travelled with a Canadian and a Mexican. We were zigzagging across Europe. The Berlin Wall at this time was still up. Within in a year, it was down. Always remember President Ronald Reagan's famous words to the Soviet Premier: "Mr Gorbachev, tear down this wall."

On the way to the German border, the famous city of Arnhem was along the way. There is a big war cemetery from the Second World War where a lot of allied servicemen are buried. This is where

THE NEXT ADVENTURE WAS STARTING TO UNFOLD

one of the last big battles between the German Panzer divisions and the allied troops was. The hotel is a museum now and was the allied headquarters then. There are displays in the underground cellars, rolling movies, and wax models of German, English and American servicemen displaying scenes of action. Outside tanks and heavy armed vehicles left there from the day the battle finished remain on display, broken and shelled from heavy fighting. (WE MUST ALWAYS REMEMBER THOSE WHO FOUGHT FOR OUR FREEDOM AS FREEDOM COMES WITH A PRICE).

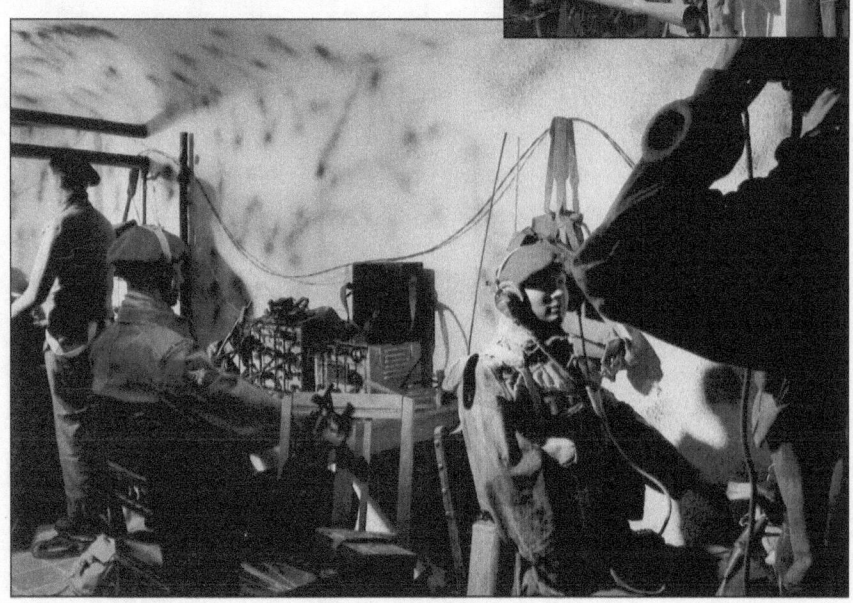

As mentioned, it was at this time I met up with a Canadian and a Mexican with a slight excursion still heading towards the German border. We hit Brussels, the capital of Belgium. We went wandering around Brussels and got lost. We had initially dumped our backpacks at the youth hostel and went walking. There was no GPS in those days. All we had was a map, which only covered a portion of the city. What's in Brussels? History, buildings, great food, French-speaking people. The international currency is controlled from here.

It had taken us a few good hours to find some sort of direction back to our hostel and some normality, meeting some people we were not so sure of along the way. We had the basic French words we could mutter to get a few directions and, yes, some very helpful people who stopped to help us. We did get to see downtown Brussels, the people and the culture. No terrorists then just a great European city. The currency then was Belgium Franks and, yes, Belgium has got a royal family. The king's portrait was on the currency at the time. (I still have some Belgium Franks). The three of us had some laughs. We stayed in Brussels for a few days before catching the wrong train and landing up in Luxembourg. Remember, I said the stations in European cities have north, south, east and west.

Luxembourg is another medieval city with historic buildings and underground tunnels. I didn't really have much time in Luxembourg, only to say that I had been there to say a few hellos. Another European city, it probably would have had a bit more to offer but I was keen to get to the German border. My friends went in a different direction.

I spoke a little German then but know more today. Bonn was the capital of West Germany then and with the wonderful upgrade of the Reichstag in Berlin after the reunification of East and West Germany, the German chancellery is again in this impressive building, having been damaged from the Second World War and the Berlin Wall going up around the back end of the building in 1960.

I love the German people, travelling through to Heidelberg, Mannheim, Koln, Black Forrest, Stuttgart, Bonn, Koblenz and passing through other cities in Germany. Also, I felt the fascination of Deutschland history, gothic buildings, colorful towns.

Deutschland hat wunderSchon

There were youth hostels in castles near the Rhine valley. When going back this time with my wife, we travelled to Salzburg, Obersalzburg, the Bavarian Alps, and Berchtesgaden (where the German dictator Adolph Hitler's mansion lies in ruins).

I don't drink but still was able to mix with friends and have a good time checking out some of the nightlife.

A man picked me up one day when hitchhiking at the top of the autobahn, thinking it was a camp platz, which is a camping ground where I wanted to go. My German must have been a little distorted as I wanted to go to Koblenz, a city situated on both banks of the Rhine. Waiting for the driver who picked me up to converse with the camping ground manager, I managed to quickly remove myself from the premises to find my own accommodation in Koblenz at a youth hostel.

I never ate much fast foods in Germany but was a frequent shopper at most supermarkets for the basic essentials. Most youth hostels then had breakfast included in the price of staying.

Germany is a place of contrast, culture, and industry, very good industry. It has some of the best technology in the world, which was worth seeing. From car manufacturing, steel structures, household appliance, and automation, the list goes on. It was all around you.

A Swedish fella and I hitchhiked at the beginning of the autobahn, alongside the Rhine River. I have never seen so many commercial boats, river cruising boats, and ships as I saw working this river. The Rhine has a very strong current so vessels one way move very quickly and of course in the opposite direction laboring against the current. Also there are these vessels going sideways across the river as well.

I saw magnificent castles and even one youth hostel was a

castle. I saw a location used for movies and another place, inland a bit, where Nazis hid stolen artefacts at the closing of World War 2.

It was forty years after World War 2 and Germany had been rebuilt. The buildings, cathedrals, monuments, museums, cafes, restaurants, tourist attractions, and manufacturing were mind boggling. It was great.

Continuing on from Germany, I hitchhiked up to Switzerland.

Deutschland Hat ein schnelles Tempo, ist aber ein groBartiger Ort fur einen Besuch. (Germany has a fast moving pace, but it is a great place to visit).

I hitchhiked around the bottom of the Alps to Switzerland, crossing the German Swiss border through the first port of call Basel. Switzerland is surrounded by mountains. I wanted to see someone playing his Alpine horn and someone else yodeling. I went searching in vain. It wasn't till a few years later that a Swiss fella came to New Zealand with his Alpine horn and gave us a few memorial moments. It was like a long smokers' pipe, except it had three parts you had to assemble. Being played, it had a deep pitch tone and he couldn't yodel.

Switzerland was expensive but was refreshing. Switzerland is well renowned for its banking, watch making, jewelry. Families live together and share houses with different levels for each family, the youngest family on the bottom floor to the grandparents on the top floor. A little different now for city dwellers.

The languages spoken are French, German, and Italian plus a little English and the currency is Swiss francs, not euros. I spent three to four days here, having been invited to stay at various people's places. It seems a long time ago. Switzerland was a neutral country in times of war. Its mountainous terrain would be a difficult country to capture. People were always escaping across the Swiss Alps to Switzerland, not the other way around, in war time.

Journeying back through the Netherlands to France, I stopped briefly and stayed with the Salvation Army minister and his family in Rotterdam. The Salvation Army in the Netherlands is called Leger Des Heils and in Germany Heils Army. Also I got to play in some of the Salvation Army brass bands as I had my cornet mouthpiece with me. That was different but music, especially brass, is music. Good workout playing though.

Travelling into Paris is the next part of the adventure.
It was on a train with no overnight accommodation. In the morning, heads were on tray tables, legs were over seats, body parts were everywhere. We pulled into the Paris train station. Well, the French can be nice and helpful when they want but difficult ninety percent of the time, especially if there is a language barrier. They understand what you are saying in English or German but play dumb and arrogant. Paris is a great city though. Paris is a vibrant city, the Eiffel Tower, the Somme River, Madame Tussauds, the restaurants, the French Rivera down the ways, the history in its buildings, the different cultures that make up France. The French are very proud people as their country was once taken from them in war nearly half a century ago at that time.

I got to drive in France in an old Renault. The countryside is interesting as well. There are farms everywhere. I kept thinking I am going to run into Renae of the English comedy TV series Allo Allo with his bartender apron and little cap on.

Back in Paris, the Eiffel Tower looks great from the top during the day and even more spectacular with lights at night. One of the disadvantages going to the toilet near the tower or anywhere at a public facility, you have to pay and someone comes and cleans up after. They may take credit cards now.

Goodbye France, Hello England

Flying from Paris to London didn't take very long, maybe less than an hour. It was a short flight. I landed at Heathrow. My English cousin was expecting me, as it was a return visit when Lisa stayed with us in New Zealand for a year previous. Lisa had eloped with a New Zealand fella months before and Lisa and Paul were just living out of London in an area called Hanwell. It was easy to catch the tube (the underground rail system around London) to the small flat. A one bedroom, lounge, kitchen upstairs flat. I got to sleep in the lounge on the couch. It was all good.

London was great. I walked and travelled via the underground tube everywhere in London and outer London. Went to Buckingham Palace and had morning tea with the Queen (only joking), did the Windsor Castle walk around the castle, watched the changing of the guards, boated down the Thames River, went to Greenwich where time begins (UTC time or as it used to be GMT), walked Regent Square, Piccadilly Circus, went to the Houses of Parliament, visited Hadley Park next to the Big Ben Clock Tower, and visited the War Memorial Museum and more. I must have stepped on all the main stations from Paddington to Marylebone, Victoria station.

One attraction I missed was the Farnbourgh Airshow, not having timed it right.

Outer London was great too. My mother had left the UK twenty-five years previously with Dad so I had a catch up with relatives from London to Yorkshire.

Lisa and Paul showed me the markets on the weekends and we also had part in sailing as mentioned on the Thames. Lisa had a brother and two sisters, whom I was able to meet except Lisa's older brother Anthony.

Another highlight in London was going to the Twickenham Rugby Ground where many of the international games are played against England. Its where the New Zealand All Blacks thrashed England on many occasions. Have to rub that one in. Later I would run around Cardiff Arms Park, the Welsh international stadium. The All Blacks

THE NEXT ADVENTURE WAS STARTING TO UNFOLD

were on a winning streak there too on many occasions.

Lisa and Paul were both working at the time. There was a time that looked tempting to be employed for a few days' work myself. Contractors were gutting the insides of these old buildings and making up market apartments for the Arabs. (Through Mum, I could work in England without a visa). However, travelling and continuing being on an adventure seemed more appealing. So travelling from London to Stockton-on-Tees in County Durham to see my Aunt and Uncle seemed more appealing. British rail were having strikes at the time but managed to avoid the disruptions.

My uncle was a Yorkshireman who had served in the Royal Navy as a Petty Officer for a period of time. Out of the navy, he had lived with his wife and family for many years in Zambia, working as a radiologist in the Kit we copper mine.

(I have a collection of stamps from Zambia when Ken and June sent mail and parcels to Mum in New Zealand). Uncle Ken, whom I had met many years earlier from a trip to New Zealand, was well-retired but was still very active and Stockton-on-Tees, which is situated near the River Tees, was well suited for Ken and Kate, his later wife.

Ken drove me through the Yorkshire Moors, drove me to Captain James Cook's old school. Stockton itself is a little country market town, having a small population of 85,000 people, plus a few more people in the wider area. Mainly, it is suited for retiring or retired persons but very pleasant. I stayed for about four days and then headed for Cornwall.

Recapping on my experience with older English people, I found they had a limited sense of humor as when watching funny movies with my uncle Ken and Kate. I must say most British humor is funny and more understandable than American humor. Anyways, to cut a long story short, I was watching a funny western movie one night, laughing my head off, and Ken couldn't understand what was so funny.

Last day of looking around Stockton-on-Tees through the village shops. It seems like nothing much changes over the years in a lot of English countryside towns.

Moving onto Wales, I travelled by train to Cardiff. One place I needed to see was Cardiff Castle, where the second night there was a military tattoo, an international military tattoo. As well as the Scotts guards, Welsh guards, Royal Marines, there were the Gurkha regiment, German regiment, pipe bands from all over the commonwealth, military displays. This was a four hour show with parachutists from one of the airborne regiments, military helicopters dropping commandos. Everything was buzzing in Cardiff. By the way, never mess with a Gurkha, they are very fast with their knives and disappearing all of a sudden as I found out on a military base in Australia years later.

The second place to see was Cardiff Arms Rugby Park. This is where you hear the Welsh singing in support of national teams. (They pretty much need the singing when Wales' national rugby team faces the New Zealand All Blacks). Here I ran around Cardiff Arms Park.

That night in Cardiff, I met a young couple, got to talking with them, and stayed a couple of nights with them. I ended up walking around part of Cardiff in those two days. One thing that was enjoyable travelling around the UK was that people were really inquisitive and wanted to know about you, where you were from (most guessed my accent), and were happy to help and were even happy to show you around their towns or counties. In the UK, the weather has an affect on people physiologically. If the weather was bleak and raining, people were generally miserable, which was generally a few months of the year.

The weather in the UK in the summer months had been wonderful during the weeks visiting the country.

Leaving Cardiff, I trained down to the South of the UK to Penzance and Lands' End in Cornwall. Note that everywhere you go, I mean from county to county, the accents are very different. Cornwall was no exception. Penzance was where the series *Poldark* was filmed on the coastal town. Growing up on the beach and coming to the coastal areas of the UK just gave you the freshness of the sea air. Penzance and Lands' End are more holiday and fishing areas with rugged coastlines. People here are pretty conservative but happy. Many things don't change in this part of the world for years, for example, houses, routines, people's habits. But in saying that, people are great and welcoming. You have to learn some local slang or colorful terms as they spoke their native Cornish. I only spent a few days here, having registered in a friendly backpackers. From here, I moved to Portsmouth. There is a large navy presence here as Her Majesty's Royal Navy has one of her bases based out of Portsmouth. There was an armada of navy ships coming and going at this time. Portsmouth is roughly 200 km from Penzance, which is still in the south of the UK. The few days being in Portsmouth, I checked out the beaches as the weather was great. They had a sea pool here. When the tide came in, it filled up the pool and as the tide went out, you could swim in the pool. I believe they have wave generators working on the tide coming in. Paddles on a generator will rotate one way and when the tide goes out, paddles reverse cycle and go the other way, generating power. The Europeans use this principle as well.

Food was pretty traditional, especially if you went to pubs for a pub meal. Meat pies, mashed potatoes and peas were always on the menu. Again, as the name suggests, Portsmouth is another coastal city and a very outdoor place in the summer months. I was only here two days, then took a train back to London to grab a few things and then travelled up to Scotland.

Leaving London once again on my British rail pass to train up to Edinburgh via Aberdeen, I got caught in the train strikes and was delayed or the train I was on was delayed. There had been an international Scout Jamboree somewhere in the UK and we had a train load of Scottish Scouts in their kilts, singing away very happily. Also on the train were a few colonels of the Confederate Air Force from the USA (later renamed the Commemorative Air Force in 2002), all paid to be colonels who had been flying their phantom jets for an airshow. Each one of these guys had their own professions. One guy was a milkman, another a teacher, another a bus driver back home, all flying ex-military restored jets. This is a story in itself. I have read about this historic, privately-owned Air Force, where they have many restored vintage aircraft that they restored to flying conditions. Maybe one day I could become an honourary colonel in the Confederacy.

We made Edinburgh that evening very late and once again there was no accommodation open. An Austrian couple and I teamed up and decided to roll out mats and sleeping bags on the tiled Edinburgh railway station, inside of course. Unfortunately for us, the police on duty that night didn't take too kindly to our sleeping arrangements and in a broad Scottish accent told us to clear off. We asked if they would be most accommodating and allow us to use their cells for the night at the station as no hostels or motels were open at that time. They didn't see the funny side to that either. We did eventually find some under cover shelter not too far from the station and managed to set up camp discretely for a few hours. It was quite cool that night and it wasn't even winter.

Edinburgh, the Scottish capital, the bag pipes—the world's most annoying instrument—the kilts, the dancing, the parades, the food and the history. This is where my history began from Robert the Bruce king of Scotland, an ancestor way back in the Stewart family history. His statue is engraved at the entrance of Edinburgh castle. An old wall around the old city was originally designed to keep the Scots in and the English out. When they built the new part of Edinburgh, the Scots did not want to move and so the first Scotsman fell for a bribe, that is, some bottles of whisky for him to be relocated into this new area. I was told this on a local tour. Whether this is true or not, I will leave to your imagination.

Edinburgh was a fun city and this was summer, not the harsh winter which would have changed my outlook on staying in a cold place. Walking into Edinburgh castle, which is like a big fortress up on a rock overlooking Edinburgh, I was amazed to see a smaller courtyard where they have a bigger military tattoo than I expected, but nonetheless, the preparations were being made for the annual event. I can remember walking around as many areas as were open to the public in the castle. The Scots are great inventors and have proved so over the centuries, working with very little. They have created and invented many things. Alexander Graham Bell initiated the first telephone, a Scotsman invented the TV in the 1930s, a Scotsman discovered penicillin and there are many more inventions they have given to make the world a better place. The Scots also have fought many battles with the English over the centuries, having won some great victories and having some great defeats. It was the last famous battle of Culloden where the English managed to lure the Scots from the Highlands and ambush them, defeating them. I remember also going to that very place. (Missed the Edinburgh military tattoo by two days. On bucket list for my next trip).

Having walked down Princess Street, the road itself runs from the castle into Edinburgh. I walked into a kilt shop and asked whether it would be possible to have a photo taken in the Royal Stewart tartan kilt, complete with black jacket and sporum, white socks, shoes and dagger. The man looked at me and said, "Laddy, you have to buy the kilt first." I was a little guttered but a shrewd Scotsman would not see his products taken advantage of. By the way, 600 Scottish pounds was the going rate and that was just the kilt. The Stewart tartans are the royal, the dress, the hunting, and the mourning.

The Scots have some very interesting foods and if you like haggis, tripe or anything that comes out a cow, you will certainly find it on most menus. The British are not far behind as my mother grew up eating tripe, brains, tongue, ox-heart, etc. That was the first few days in Edinburgh, complete with bus tour.

Next stop I went to the school where they filmed *Chariots of Fire*, the story of the Scottish Olympic runner in the 1923 Olympic Games who won the 100 meters and 200 meters sprint. He maintained his principles and never ran on the Sabbath due to his conviction of honoring God. God honored him and he went on to win medal after medal. Eric Lydel was his name. Not long after these games, he became a missionary in China, educating and reaching out to the Chinese people. Eric was eventually interned by the Japanese prior to Second World War, dying of an illness in a Japanese camp. GREAT MOVIE. I RECOMMEND IT.

I am a Scotsman at heart, though I think it would be very cold to live and work there, although my heritage is still Scottish. The amazing backdrops such as the Lochs, the Highlands, the Glens, the castles and castle ruins are just breathtaking, and its history contains centuries of history and continual wars where the Scots defended their part of the British Isles.

And if you don't know the Scottish national anthem, you will be reminded of O FLOWER OF SCOTLAND.

This song is talking about how the Scots kicked the English out.

As the song goes, THERE WILL ALWAYS BE AN ENGLAND WITH SCOTLAND RIGHT BEHIND.

The last part of my Scottish trip up the Isle was to Inverness where the Loch Ness Monster is continually being looked for. I myself still believe prehistoric monsters have lived even up till recent times and Inverness is a very deep loch which opens to the North Sea. There is a castle ruin at the head of the lake called Urquhart Castle. It overlooks the loch. There is a village near this. All I can remember up there is that it is very cold and very green. Sometimes you wonder how people could have survived in places like that over the centuries but people adapt, even to places like Northern Canada, North America, and Mongolia where some of my friends work now in conditions where temperatures are minus 30 degrees. So I suppose 18 degrees minus is not too bad.

There are many more interesting parts to Scotland and its people and just like the Welsh, the Scots are as shrewd as they may be. The Welsh are a bit more hot headed but they are very hospitable.

Returning from Inverness by train down the other side of the

British Isles, I passed through Glasgow, Bristol, and Swindon, stopping briefly. The Glasgow Rangers soccer team were not playing at this time, which was too bad as I would have loved to have gone to a home game. Next time.

Making my way back to London on British Rail, this time no strikes and we arrived on time in London. My trip to the British Isles ended at Heathrow Airport a night after returning from Yorkshire, Wales, and Scotland.

Leaving the United Kingdom and flying across the Atlantic to North America.

The Big Scare
On the flight out of London, something out of the ordinary happened. Won't tell you what airline I was on but we had a suspected bomb on board. A red bag had gone missing and it was believed to be hidden under some seats on this aircraft. We didn't know this until we were climbing over the Atlantic.

That bag had thought to have been placed under the seat I was sitting on and the crew came down and asked us to leave our seats whilst they pulled the row of seats apart. There was a little panic at first until we had been assured by the crew everything would be OK. Obviously it had been reported as an unidentified bag. The flight continued and we did land safely in Los Angeles. I think the plane was searched again on the ground. The crew apologised to us for the inconvenience and said every precaution had been taken. One thing I do know and give God the glory for is continued guidance and knowing his angels are there with me. Over the years, I have travelled thousands upon thousands of air miles and he has proven time and time again through his word that he is faithful.

Arriving in Los Angeles in the early hours of the morning, I could not remember what day it was. I met up with a fella who worked at Los Angeles International Airport. His name was Paul and Paul had no fixed abode, he stayed at a different friend's house every night.

Well, we got to talking about where I was from and what he did at the airport, just general chatter, and by morning he suggested we go down to the country club where he had breakfast most days. We freshened up and had pancakes for breakfast with some coffee. We talked a bit more about the Los Angeles area. He then dropped me back at the airport around 8:00 am to catch the flight to Toronto International. I never saw him again after that, just have a photo of him getting into his car and driving off. I was meeting up with my seafaring friend from the Canadian Navy, the fella who had sailed on the Canadian ship to New Zealand three years earlier. When meeting up with Daniel later, I found he had just been transferred to the Canadian Army.

I had bought this ticket with Republic Airlines outside the USA for $350 unlimited travel anywhere in the US on standby. You had to be under twenty-three years. I was told this ticket could be used to fly across the border into Canada with the same airline, but finding a dispute had arisen between the Canadian Government and the airline, I was allowed to use my standby ticket anywhere and everywhere in the USA only. It was still OK. It only meant I would have to fly right across to Detroit and catch a shuttle bus from Detroit Airport to cross the border from America to Canada. This I did and crossed the bridge to a Canadian city called Windsor. From there to Toronto International Airport where Daniel had arranged to meet me.

It was an overnight bus and again I happened to meet up with some other backpackers going home to Toronto. One of these backpackers was a young lady who told me this situation she got into in the Black Forest in Germany. This was a very dumb thing to do for a young women; even for a young male, it wouldn't be the smartest idea. This is Vicky. Vicky had been on an overnight bus somewhere going through the Black Forest. There were only a few people on this bus and there was this one fella she said looked disturbing. Vicky got off this bus at a stop in the dark and this fella got off as well. She said she was so scared, she dropped her backpack and ran into the forest. She lay on the ground all night, hearing footsteps walking all around, presumably the man looking for her. In the morning there was no one to be seen. Vicky then moved on, end of story. Not a bright thing to do.

Anyway it was a two hour drive as I remember from Detroit to Toronto International Airport. I phoned Daniel where and when I was going to be and in what terminal. The bus dropped me off at terminal 28. Daniel would pick me up within an hour and a half as he had to drive in from his base CBF Borden Barry Ontario. I grabbed my backpack and went down to the end of the terminal, placed it on the floor, and lay down with my head on my pack. It was about 8 pm at this time and Daniel came in his military uniform. Daniel had forgotten what I looked like. He paged me as he is standing right in front of me. To his surprise, I jumped up right in front of him. We had a great laugh.

We talked all the way back to camp. Daniel never stops talking and he was funny good sense of humor just like me. Daniel introduced me to all his superiors, officers his regiment personal everyone he could think of. I somehow got to know them all. Daniel had got permission for me to stay on the base for the last few days he was at work and had then arranged to take leave and drive up North.

CBF Borden was a huge base with military airport, shopping centers, every sport center you could think of as well as fast food outlets and of course military accommodation, parade grounds and military stores. It was like a center inside the city of Barry except it was military. This was summer in Canada and believe me the winters are very harsh.

We went sailing on Lake Simcoe on the shores of Barry, Ontario. This lake freezes over in the winter and you can actually skate on it. We sailed on this lake with some of Daniel's friends and their boat. I had been wearing a pair of New Zealand flag shorts at the time; eventually, when I jumped in the water for a swim, my shorts were hoisted up the mast as if to fly the New Zealand flag. We sailed the whole afternoon.

Daniel introduced me to some other close friends off base in the city of Barry. One particular older fella we called Uncle Burt, an Englishmen who had immigrated with his wife and family to Ontario back in the late 1950s and early 60s. Burt was in seventies then and very active; he loved to teach brass music to young people in the Salvation Army. I always remember him moving around fast and getting things done, either cleaning up at home or in the community. He was a great fella. His wife Marion, just a few years younger, was so funny. You could have some great laughs and also some great conversations with her. She made every situation sound funny, to a point. Even my accent to her was funny. We got on great and thinking back now, I really miss those types of people. That generation has died off and we are now the generation behind them. The week we spent with them was great.

Daniel finished his work on base and we drove up North to an old English fort. I think it was called Fort Henry. The Canadian military still uses the fort today for military displays, utilizing trainee officer cadets in old English style infantry uniforms, parading, giving mock battles, using old cannons, and firing old muskets in the front and rear formation. It was quite good entertainment. We were able to use one of the military dorms on this base that had big military dorms and the personnel were out on exercise. If you can imagine a row of beds down one side and a row on the other with the beds perfectly made. The two nights we were there, Daniel had one end of the dorm and I had the other because he snored something terrible. Well, the echoes from his snoring in that room seemed to vibrate off all four walls; even a pillow would not suppress his snoring. The remedy for such a case was standing over him and dropping some grapes into his mouth one by one. I heard a series of grunts as he tried to consolidate the grapes without choking. He got the message and I think he slept on his side for the rest of the night.

We drove from there to Ottawa, the capital of Canada, and decided to take a full tour of the Houses of Parliament. Yes, they also

have a Changing of the Guards parade like they do in Britain for the Queen at Windsor Castle and Buckingham Palace, quite impressive as they too have their black busby bear skin hats with ceremonial scarlet tunics. So we watched the parades going through the Houses of Parliament, saw the debating chamber and as much as we were allowed to see in the two hours before the tour dispersed. Daniel and I somehow landed up in a press conference where a cabinet minister was being interviewed. We were right at the front so we pulled out notebooks and pens and pretended to take notes as questions were being asked. Daniel even started taking photos like the rest of the journalists. We still have the photos. And then we left as quietly as we came.

We went from there to a summer camp on a lake. There were lots of people our age at the time, including these two girls who kept hassling both Daniel and me. We had a surprise coming for them. We had paddled a Canadian canoe out on the lake, unfortunately these two lovely ladies decided to join us. They were OK looking but to prevent them tailing us in the future, we sank their canoe and they had to swim back to shore. We got called all sorts of fun names after that (not derogatory though). They saw the funny side as well. Ontario has many lakes and you can picture a movie set with this big lake with log cabins in the middle of summer. This same lake would have been frozen over in the middle of winter with a few ice huts for fishing.

After five days at the camp and cooking marsh-mellows around the fire at night, we parted company with those fun young people. Daniel and I drove to Niagara Falls initially on the Canadian side where the horseshoe is. We went as close as we could to the Falls, very commercialised. We didn't go on the boat, the Lady of the Mist, which moved right up to the falls. Instead we watched movies of daredevils who had gone over in barrels and survived. Also there had been people game enough to tightrope walk across the top as they were filmed. We found out the flow of water can be controlled when necessary and also helicopters fly over patrolling the area for at risk people venturing out to the stupid things.

From the Canadian side, Daniel drove me across the border to the American side of the Falls, which is not as impressive. Across the border bridge was a city called Buffalo. I had spent two weeks with Daniel travelling across Northern Ontario and would be back a year later in the winter to drive right across Canada in the middle of winter.

I met this nice Canadian girl in Barry, Ontario and didn't really want to go. When Daniel dropped me off at Buffalo International Airport, I started to use my air pass around the states. Buffalo was the second airport, as I had flown out of Los Angeles to Detroit, Michigan first. At this point, I kept thinking about Lisa and at every opportunity, I rang her to tell her where I was and the plans I had made in those American cities. Lisa wanted me to come back sometime soon as she liked me a lot. I knew that if my air pass was not used for more adventures, my journey would stop. But it would take me back to see Lisa later.

In a month, my air pass flew me into around thirty-five states: the people I met and stayed with, the amusement parks visiting, the rocket sites I went to see, I even stood on the very place where JFK was shot in Dallas (one of the best Democratic presidents the USA ever had). I flew over and around the Grand Canyon.

I met up with another Paul in Wisconsin and we drove to where the Mississippi, the Black Fire and the Black Hawk Rivers meet. I think these names are right. I went to the first Space Rocket Centre in Alabama, crisscrossed to Washington DC, over to Washington State to Seattle to see the Space Needle there. In some places, I stayed in youth hostels where I would ring Lisa. There was the one time my backpack went to San Francisco from Minneapolis and I went from Minneapolis to Los Angeles. Republic Airlines didn't have a direct flight from Los Angeles to San Francisco so I had to fly all the way back to Minneapolis to San Francisco to collect my backpack, which had been damaged. It wasn't a problem, this air pass worked great, I was just annoyed about the damage. San Francisco was great though. The Golden Gate Bridge, Alcatraz in the Bay, Fisherman's Wharf, the steep streets walking up and trams moving up those streets as well to pick you up and drop you off, being able to use binoculars to observe ships coming and going in the San Francisco Bay. There's still lots more to see. I remember staying in a backpackers in downtown Frisco and walking the streets in the city. Just had to be careful where you went though.

When landing in Seattle, Washington, Daniel had suggested that I take the old steamer, the Princess Margaret, across to Vancouver Island in Canada to see his mother. This old girl, I mean the ferry, was very majestic looking. The capital of the island is Victoria and it's where the Queen Mother often stayed. You can sail from Seattle or Vancouver by car ferries. There is also a big Canadian Navy presence on the island. Daniel had previously been based here.

Daniel's mother Lorna I did get to see and stepfather also. Daniel had a big family with two sisters, one older and one younger, and two adopted First Nations sisters. The sisters were really given a hard time in Canada because of their color. Lorna loved those girls but she was also given a hard time by the community for caring for them, but she was a very compassionate women, stern but firm, and these girls did very well in achieving. One if not two worked for Air Canada as ground staff as I remember which was a big achievement for them.

The weather on the west coast of Canada was also a lot milder than the east coast so a bit more sunlight hours. Vancouver Island would be a place I would revisit a year later, this time in the winter.

Vancouver Island is an island full of forestry and Indian preservation. The economy over the years had deteriorated to a point that many businesses had closed down in the late 1980s. A group of artists had decided they could help bring some tourism back by painting magnificent pictures on different buildings with a foot trail to each building in the main center. These pictures were of Indians in their native dress, people building and constructing the township in the 1800s, men working in the forestry during that period of time. I still have pictures of these events as it became an international tourist attraction.

Having stayed with Lorna and John for those few days and driving around the island, I sailed back on the steamer to Seattle and resumed my flying around the USA.

I flew to Dallas and Fort Worth and travelled to the monument on the grassy knolls where President Kennedy was shot. Again I stayed at youth hostels and walked the streets of Dallas, saw where they filmed some of the western movies and more. Texas is a very rich state in black gold (oil) and big guns as it is not a crime to carry a gun as long as it is licensed. It is also known for its big steaks. Never order large meals at a restaurant or diner, as you will never get through it. I found Texas to be full of friendly people and helpful people. I would have loved to catch up with all the colonels from the Confederate Air Force I had met in Scotland but ran out of time. I found also as a Kiwi you had to talk slower for the average Texan to understand you as we have a habit of speaking too fast.

From Dallas, I flew to Memphis and saw Elvis Presley's Graceland, then through to Atlanta, Georgia, Washington DC (I saw The White House, Space Museum, and anything that had fast moving machinery). I took a train in and out of Washington DC and back to the airport.

I flew from Washington to Huntsville, Alabama, sometimes called Rocket City. I went here to the US Space Rocket Center, NASA's Marshall Space Flight Center and the US Army Aviation and Missile Command. This is where the first rocket building programs started after WW2 with the German rocket scientist Werner Von Braun who built the space rockets, sending the astronaut into space and landing spacecraft on the moon. He had previously built the V1 and dreaded V2 rockets for Nazi Germany. There were state parks, museums, and gardens to see. Then I moved on.

Next port of call, back to Los Angeles where I met up with Rob, a contact through the Salvation Army. By this time, my finances were running low so my air pass came in handy for breakfast, lunch, dinner, and sleep. I flew everywhere else in the US to accommodate myself.

In Los Angeles, I was able to stay with Rob in his unit for a few days. We spent one day in Disneyland out at Anaheim which was great being a kid again. Lapped up all the rides from roller coasters, Adventureland, Frontierland, Pirates of the Caribbean, Space Mountain, the whole day was full. The following day we were at Santa Monica beach, one of the great surfing beaches, followed by travelling up to Long Beach, California and to the Korean shrine that overlooks Los Angeles over the smog.

The last few days, I went out to Santiago to the navy base and walked around the Queen Mary, which is now a floating hotel, not an ocean going ship. The Queen Mary was used for protection of the Royal family during WW2. It still had anti-aircraft guns on the back end. Right next to the Queen Mary was Howard Hughes' Spruce Goose under a hangar. This was the biggest plane ever built as a troop transport aircraft and only flew once off the water. (In recent years, it has been dismantled, moved and reassembled somewhere else.) We didn't see all but some of the Santiago Zoo on the last day.

I drove back to LA and the following day flew the long haul flight back to New Zealand. All in all, I travelled for nearly three months. I travelled something like thirty-two thousand air miles; visited nine European countries, including the British Isles; walked with my backpack down the Rhine Valley and through the Netherlands, and up the Welsh and Scottish parts of the British Isles, completing three hundred kilometres (km) of walking and riding a push bike; landed in India for twenty hours on the way over to Europe; flew to and from thirty-five states of the USA; drove two thousand km in

Canada; and drove another two thousand km on the east coast of the USA and around another fifteen hundred km in the Wisconsin area of the USA. I returned a year later to travel even further across the North American continent as I will tell later in the book. The many people I had met along the way were not only friends and family but strangers who welcomed me into their homes, some having kept in contact with me and some that I have never seen again.

I was jet-lagged for a few days, but that was only the beginning of what was to come.

Arriving Back in Kiwi Land

Two weeks of being back in New Zealand and prior to my overseas trip, I had paid for my ground theory course for my commercial pilot licence. When I had returned home to New Zealand, I literally had no money but after those two weeks of being home, I packed my bags, said goodbye to Mum and Dad, and drove my little Austin mini north to Auckland. It had cost $800 at the time to do this theory course of five to six pilot subjects at a flying school in South Auckland, New Zealand. My family friends in South Auckland (Papakura) had taken me as a border at the time and I was very grateful for them. Dan and Julie lived near Ardmore Airport, where flying schools and training aircraft operated from, away from Auckland International Airport. My trusted push bike I had brought with me rode five km to and from Ardmore Airport most days except if it rained. I did this for three months and worked hard to pass my commercial pilot's theory subjects. There were manuals on aviation law, navigational flight planning, aerodynamics, meteorology, and aircraft performance. It also touched on human factors, which now is a full subject in itself.

We actually went to the Royal New Zealand Air Force training base Hobsonville at the time to understand the significance of hypoxia, which is the lack of oxygen to the brain when there is a decompression of aircraft at high altitudes or when a pilot flies at altitudes above 14000 feet with no oxygen.

THE NEXT ADVENTURE WAS STARTING TO UNFOLD

We were placed in a pressurised chamber with oxygen masks on and were taken up to the equivalent of 35,000 feet one by one. We were told to take oxygen masks off and with a clipboard to write, counting down backwards from one hundred in a series of seven. (The symptoms of hypoxia are lips turning blue) Everyone is affected differently but when you start counting backwards in sevens, your brain with less oxygen makes all your responses to become less responsive to a point you don't function properly. You cannot even think what number comes next. It was at this point that your oxygen masks were placed back on. I did happen to see a fella pass out within seconds at 35,000 feet and his mask was quickly placed back on. Without oxygen or a limited supply, you could be dead in minutes. Many accidents have occurred when pilots have mistakenly not effectively pressurised aircraft or flown without oxygen at high altitudes and it only takes approximately three to four minutes of no oxygen before you can go unconscious and never wake up.

We were also shown the effects of your sensors. By sensors, I mean your eyes, ears and central balance. One of the fellas was placed in a revolving chair, blindfolded, and told to place his arms straight out and thumbs pointing up. The chair was spun in one direction and stopped. Immediately when stopped, his sensors gave his body the sensation he was turning in the other direction and his thumbs pointed in that direction as he was still under a blindfold. The point of this exercise is that you have to rely totally on instrumentation when flying in clouds with your primary instruments, your artificial horizon, altimeter, turn and slip indicator. Your sensors can give you the impression you are flying straight and level when in fact you are in a descending turn. There were a few other experiments involving symptoms of hyperventilation and how to compensate for that.

We had an A Cat instructor taking the navigation course. His name I will mention was Brian Cox. He was a very short man with a wealth of experience in the fifty years he had been flying. Brian was a wartime pilot who flew the Corsair dive bombers in the Pacific

Theatre and after WW2 was on the J Force team that went to Japan in peacekeeping after 1945 and the surrender of the Japanese forces.

Brian had photos in his log book with many samurai swords surrendered by Japanese military offices and he also attended some of the war crimes trials.

Anyways getting back to flying, Brian was nineteen-years-old when he flew on combat with the RNZAF (New Zealand Air Force) and he told this story. His commanding officer emphasised the point that in any conflict, you should always keep your wing man in sight. This day their squadron was over Japanese territory and one of their own was shot down. The fella bailed out with some wounds as the squadron were strafing Japanese boats to try and protect this fella. Eventually, the Japanese picked this guy up and he died from his wounds in a Japanese field hospital. The rest of the squadron had to return as they were running low on fuel but got caught in a tropical cyclone on the way back. Brian always remembered the words of his commanding officer to always keep your wing man in sight. Brian and his wing man were the only ones who made it back to base. It wouldn't be till about twenty years later I read Brian's story in the New Zealand Herald.

There were about twenty-three of us in this class with many different backgrounds. We had helicopter pilots, fixed wing pilots, engineers and prospective airline pilots who even had background trades like my own in electricity, or air traffic controlling, or meteorology. One of these fellas was the son of the engineer on the Air New Zealand DC 10 that flew into Mt Erebus in Antarctica in December 1979, New Zealand's worst airline disaster ever. He and a few others became good friends for the duration of time spent at the flying school. These fellas would hire an aircraft over the weekends and for the fun of it fly low level around the North Island on cross country exercises. The other two friends who flew helicopters down the South Island would go skiing for the weekend on the mountain and come back sunburnt from the snow.

So we had a real mixture of persons as you can see from above. The course was three months full time and we had mock exams for every subject all the way through. By November, we had gone through all the elements of the weather and how to read aviation meteorological forecasts properly. We became familiar with the mechanics of flight, we formulated a flight plan and we worked out points of no return and critical points for circumstances like engine failure or having to fly on one engine. We became very familiar with New Zealand Aviation law and knowing where to find legislation when required. We learnt about balancing aircraft weight, payload, fuel and fuel consumption.

Brian Cox did pull another stunt for us before the year ended. A company from Hong Kong was making a Chinese James Bond movie and Brian was asked to be a little Chinamen flying a light aircraft. Brian was placed in a Chinese robe and his face was darkened a little and he had a long drooping mustache. Remember Brian is a wee short man and this day as not part of the stunt he came down low and flew this brand new Cessna 172 into the back of an Avis rental van and it was literally stuck in the back of the van. In the end they incorporated this scene in the movie. If it had been anyone else, the flying school would have fired them for wrecking their aircraft. (Brian did give me a copy of the photo taken on request).

End of November, we sat all the commercial aviation exams. We had two years to complete the practical flying pass, the government flight test, and be issued with a commercial pilot's license.

The following year, 1986, I went back to work at my trade to do two things: save for my practical of attaining my commercial pilot's licence and also save for my second trip back to Canada.

Before I left South Auckland at the end of 1985, two things happened: a farmer not too far from us had been shot dead one night after he was inspecting a suspected theft of farm equipment. It turned out that his wife had had a hit job done on her husband because she was having an affair with another bloke.

And in the other incident, a young fella broke into a house with a bayonet one night and got unexpectedly caught. The father got stabbed with the bayonet and the two sons smashed this fella around the head with a squash racket. In a panic, this same fella stole my push bike and clothes off the line.

Detectives interviewed me a couple of weeks later, having arrived back home in Gisborne. They wanted identification of my clothes and push bike as the scene had turned into a homicide.

This had been a very eventful year when looking back on it. I finished my apprenticeship, travelled by myself, spent three months at aviation school and stayed with my friends Dan and Julie in South Auckland. Dan and Julie had looked after me so well and it wouldn't be the last time I stayed with them at Papakura, South Auckland. In the time I spent at their place, I had also managed to keep practicing my cornet (my brass band instrument) as Dan had been actively involved in the Salvation Army banding world as well as professional bandsmen in the New Zealand Army band and we would play together. Dan had also been on overseas band tours with the national band of New Zealand. To audition for the band, you had to be pretty special. We still remain good family friends to this day.

Going home for Christmas that year had a great surprise, my Canadian friend Daniel was coming for Christmas and would be here in a week. He was one of the funniest fellas I ever knew. My parents loved him so he called them Mum and Dad and my grandparents Ma and Pa. Celebrating Christmas with no snow was a novelty for Daniel as a Canadian winter came with a dumping of snow and temperature around -20 degrees. Here he was enjoying a Christmas in the sunshine.

Daniel had travelled as he was required to in his military dress uniform and some little old lady got him mixed up with a porter. "Porter, please bring me my bags," was her request. Daniel had a great laugh. He wasn't sure if she had her glasses on or not. But he had to explain he was not a porter but on official government business. If I know Daniel, he would play this out real well to get her to believe it. He could keep a straight face to a point.

We had gone out Christmas caroling with the Salvation Army band as we often did in December. This would be on the back of trucks. Or on Sundays, we would take a vehicle out to the country farming communities and sheep or cattle stations and bring Christmas cheer with the reminder of what Christmas is all about. Daniel came along and thoroughly enjoyed this. He was just like a brother to me.

After Christmas, Daniel and I rode our faithful chariot the Austin mini (mini just like Mr Bean's car) down south. We had driven down to the Hawkes Bay (Napier Hastings) further down the east coast when we had a little engine problem. It might have been a little water in the fuel and being bush mechanics, we decided to take the point leads of the distributor cap to check underneath. That was OK till we went to connect the leads back up and managed to get them connected the wrong way. The car went better in reverse than it did forward and I cannot remember how many streets we passed in reverse to get to a service station to work out the problem.

With car fixed and points on the distributor cap the right way, we drove down to Wellington, the capital of New Zealand, and from there jumped on the interisland ferry to Picton, the top of the South Island. From there we caught the train down to Christchurch where my aunt and uncle and cousins lived. It's about a four hour drive or a six hour train trip down the Kaikora coast to Christchurch. In the middle of nowhere, the train stops and this little kid sings out, "Is this a hold up?" We were all laughing our heads off.

Anyways, we got down to Christchurch and camped at my aunt's and uncle's place. We did have a vehicle down there to roam around Christchurch, the Port Hills, Lyttelton Township and Harbor, around the city which wasn't broken at the time, around Hagley Park, New Brighton Beach, to the South Ashburton. Daniel also had a good time with my cousins and fit in real well.

We did the reverse on train back to Picton via the KiaKoras across on the ferry to Wellington, driving back up the east coast to Gisborne. Daniel spent the last week with my parents and I think my sister Marie and Fiona were there at some point as well on their Christmas break from nursing and teachers' college.

Daniel was disappointed to have to leave again and was contemplating on accessing the legal requirements to live in New Zealand. I would save up the following year and come for Christmas 1986.

That would be a very cold but interesting Christmas.

Coming Back to Reality

Having left the supply authority halfway through the last year, I started to do some freelancing electrical work for my father in his construction business. For a year, I was wiring outhouses, rewiring rented properties, and sometimes painting inside and outside of houses. Around August 1986, I picked up electrical work at the freezing works as a shift electrician and now was able to raise some more finance for a trip to Canada at the end of year and save for my commercial training.

There was still a minimum number of hours that was required to meet the commercial flight test and that was two hundred hours total plus minimum fifty hours cross country flying, so many hours instrument flying, and I think about ten hours night flying. So as I was at home, I was building up my hours as much as I could on solo cross countries or flying dual with other pilots or instructors to get my hours up. The full pilot's courses now at a flying school costs between $150,000 to $200,000 if you want to make a commercial pilot and have multi-engine instrument ratings followed by a flight instructors course. And then maybe someone will employ you in the general aviation to instruct or fly charter operations again to build up hours for the minimum requirements for an airline. After that comes airline transport subjects, which is a full course of six subjects based around a heavy jet, example, a Boeing 747.

As you can see, there is a lot of time and effort (not to mention money) to becoming a commercial/airline transport pilot.

I did as I recall learn from two serious events during that time. One, I flew cross country from Gisborne to Wellington with my dad, and approached Wellington Airport with my landing chart upside down. I did not realise this till the tower told an Air New Zealand F27 to abort take off then I realised my mistake with an anxious controller on the radio. I was told to phone the tower when on ground. By the way, this was my first flight solo into Wellington and probably the only serious mistake I made flying in New Zealand airspace. The second event was flying a group of people from Gisborne to Rotorua, a direct track across. The weather pattern had changed and a cold front was passing through, which brought showers and thunderstorms. I made the decision to go around this weather pattern but the speed at which the front was traveling meant I landed inside the weather and got caught in the up and down drafts and some hail. I had to make an emergency landing at an unused airfield at the top of the cape with my passengers in the pouring rain, I might add. Because of the wind element, I landed hard and set off the emergency locator beacon. I could hear the beacon signal coming through my head set. Having landed the plane and shutdown the engine, I quickly opened up the tail section of plane and switched off the ELB (emergency locator beacon) immediately after making contact with the nearest air traffic unit. Gisborne air traffic controllers had picked up the emergency signal and were going to alert the search and rescue. Fortunately, I was able to cancel the alert.

The owner of the aircraft was not too pleased either. My passengers stayed the night at the hotel and were transported by car the next day to their destination. A day or so later, I flew aircraft back to point of hire. This all happened before becoming a licensed commercial pilot. These were valuable learning experiences for later years.

Most pilots if not all have had some real learning curves as they have progressed through flight careers. They would be lying if they had not.

During September 1986, there had been a national strike at all meat works around New Zealand. Us tradies did not have to go out on strike but to support the other unions, a decision was made to join them. This went on for five weeks and in the end I made the decision to look for another electrical job. Out of curiosity, I applied for the Royal Engineer Corp in the New Zealand Army and to my surprise was quickly accepted because of my trade. Thinking to myself is this what I really wanted to do, I turned the opportunity down as the end of the year was coming and my Canadian infantryman was expecting me back in Canada. So was Lisa.

When you have no commitments or family, you can move around a bit and I certainly did that. I wasn't saying that in a selfish way as I have always wanted to do and help others that struggle in life. But fun is fun too and when you have someone else who is just as funny as you are, it can either be a recipe for disaster or make something extremely funny happen. I preferred the latter and that was me and Daniel.

I am not sure what my quiet mother thought of my attacks. My sisters thought I needed to grow up. But my philosophy is if you can laugh at yourself and make someone else laugh at the same time, is that not a good thing?

Towards the end of the year, I was able to increase my flying hours, which also had come from friends who wanted me to fly them from point A to point B and also through electrical contracts, I was able fly to work. The year had gone and I was on my way back to Canada, this time in the winter months.

The Flight Back to Canada

15th December 1986, I flew to Toronto via Fiji and Los Angeles on Air New Zealand and Air Canada. The temperature in Toronto was -20 degrees with a wind chill on top. It felt like being in an ice cube.

Daniel was there waiting for me and gave me a military snow jacket with a hood attached, seeing I was a little cold. We drove straight back to his military base, talking all the way. At this point he was in the Airforce so he started in the Canadian navy, was transferred to the Army and now is in the Air Force. CBF Borden, the military base, hadn't changed except there was snow all around instead of sunshine and warm air. Not sure how my security clearance was validated but I had no problems getting on and off base under Daniel's supervision.

This was an interesting Christmas as this time my cornet was with me and living on Daniel's base in the middle of winter gave me some time to practice. Daniel had this one bunk apartment and my sleeping arrangements for the first three nights was on a blowup mattress. I had the luxury of choosing between two, only to be told that one of them had a slow leak. Well 2 am the next morning, I found out the mattress had a slow leak. I woke up on a hard floor. Daniel laughed his head off.

2 am the following morning, the military decided to have a fire drill. It had been snowing, it was cold and personnel opened their doors, only to find no fire. They went back to bed. For me, I couldn't sleep after that and I went for a walk in my long johns and jacket.

This was on the Thursday and on the Friday, I stayed at my friends Burt and Marion's place in Barry. Remember my friends Burt and Marion from last time. Well, Burt had arranged for me to stand the kettles in the shopping mall and actually get paid for the days doing it. The kettle for the Salvation Army is a big copper bowl where people put money to donate for Christmas. I wasn't just going to stand there all day around a pot so out came my cornet and I played Christmas carols in my Salvation Army band uniform and white hat, making it worthwhile. The music shops cottoned on to this and in the end we had a jam session with keyboards and acoustics, playing anything that was suitable.

This little old lady, seeing me wearing a white hat, comes up to me and says, "The Salvation Army hiring Marines now?" I said, "We just borrowed some." Even the local newspaper got in the act and I had my photo taken as the "Kiwi Christmas performer." Well if you are being paid for doing something you might as well make the most of it. The kettles were set up in four shopping malls and I played in all of them and outside one bottle store where my mustache froze and had ice crystals hanging off it.

A few days before Christmas, Daniel decided we needed to have our photographs taken by a military photographer in full military dress uniform. Daniel suggested I wear his Army dress uniform and he would wear his Air Force dress uniform. My first reaction to that was I am impersonating a non-commissioned officer and that's illegal. Then I thought about it and yes, I was a non-commissioned officer in Air Force cadets in New Zealand so I didn't feel too bad about that after all.  We rocked up at the military photographers, Daniel in his Air Force blue and me in Army green. Fortunately, we were roughly the same size and nothing looked out of place. Mr Photographer looked at the names on both uniforms and, seeing they were both the same, asked if we were brothers and we said, "Yes, of course." We were like brothers. Still have these photos today.

Well, we got through that and Christmas was upon us. We had Christmas with all Burt's and Marion's family, including his English sister, Aunt Jane. Jane would have been in her early 80s like Burt and she had a funny laugh. Daniel said jokingly he had a dream the other night about Aunt Jane and the song came to mind, THE OLD GREY MARE AINT WHAT SHE USED TO BE. All the families cracked up, laughing.

In North America, they have a furnace in the basements of their houses to adequately warm every part of the house during the winter months. Outside in the mornings you can find your car buried in snow or your driveway completely under snow if it snowed hard the previous night or day. There were times we gave a hand in

THE NEXT ADVENTURE WAS STARTING TO UNFOLD

clearing the snow and ice on Burt and Marion's driveway. Snow is great when it's fresh but when it becomes mushy and the dampness gets through your skin, it gets uncomfortable.

I did meet up with Lisa for a short time again and we did stay in touch. Later on I did apply for permanent residence in Canada but was not accepted as I did not require refugee status. Thinking back, Lisa would have sponsored me on refugee status if she could have. She had fallen for me and I think was a little heartbroken when I was not allowed to stay permanently. Lisa became a police woman in the Canadian Mounted Police and eventually got married. Somehow you don't forget about the people in life who had been close to you at one point and who knows may cross paths at some point again.

After Christmas, Daniel got me involved in a military skiing expedition. Now this was going to be fun as we had some crazy women in his squad. These women were the first on the ski chair lift and were halfway up the mountain when the hydraulics on the motor housing broke down, spraying hydraulic fluid everywhere. These woman just panicked and they eventually had to be lowered by wire ladders. We hadn't got on the lift when this happened and we didn't get covered in hydraulic oil either. Some of the fellas standing nearby did. The women all got down eventually and we did manage to get up the mountain.

The next part was funny. Daniel and I had a competition to see who could wind up our competition, which happened to be some lovely young ladies. These were the skiing instructors. Pretending my skiing was not very good, I asked if they could give me some instruction; they really believed me. They showed me every position they could think of and suggested that I take it very slowly. Well, every position nearly came to the point of tripping them up. It was very hard to keep a straight face. In the end, to their surprise, I went flying down the mountain and, going round the bend, nearly went into a snow plow coming up the other way. I made a quick turn and progressively skied down the mountain. I'm not sure if the two military personnel were surprised or a little anxious that I had gone down the hill out of sight. They did come looking in the end and we had a few laughs down the bottom. These lovely ladies saw the funny side and thought it was hilarious, they could not believe I had sucked them in. It  was a fun day and we were very tired and wet by the day's end. We made it back to base and many of Daniel's regiment or squadron as he was in the Air Force were getting used to me being around. Most of Daniel's colleagues liked Daniel being around as he gave them a sense of happiness; like me, he could make a funny situation out of something serious. Even Daniel's commanding officers had to restrain themselves from laughing at some of Daniel's attics and hold their respect as his superior.

Daniel had bought a brand new car after his Volkswagen rabbit had died on a freeway. The motto of the company was WE WILL TRADE YOUR CAR IN ANYWHERE ANY PLACE FOR A BRAND NEW OLDSMOBILE. Daniel accepted their offer and the car sales company had to live to their agreement and go and pick his blown up Volkswagen on a freeway for his new Cutlass Oldsmobile Supreme two-door car. We drove this car nearly 4500 km from Toronto to Vancouver in three days.

We left Barrie, Ontario early on a Thursday morning. So we drove down through Detroit, up over across Lake Michigan and across to St Paul's, then Duluth, Minnesota up to Winnipeg across to Brandon then to Regina where they train the Canadian Mounted Police, then up to Swift Current, through to Calgary, then through the Canadian Rockies, Banff, Kamloops then Vancouver. Through the Rockies, there were cars iced over in ditches. Having chains on made the difference to stay on the road except we didn't have any chains on either. Daniel and I alternated driving and sleeping, stopping where we had to for meals and toilet breaks. So all in all, we had travelled 4387 km one way through the USA and across Canada from Barrie, Ontario to Vancouver. Reaching Vancouver, we stopped and called in to see Daniel's older sister before catching the ferry to Vancouver Island to spend a few days with his mother Lorna. Daniel's family, especially Lorna, had been into breeding horses on the mainland and his older sister had continued on with the stud farm when Lorna retired. It was a quick overnight visit in Vancouver and then we sailed across to Vancouver Island on the car ferry the following morning.

The next morning, we drove the car off the ferry and around to Lorna's new place. Daniel knocked on the door to his mother's surprise. She closed the door, she was all excited, not expecting Daniel and I to have driven all this way and sailed across to the island. Lorna made a big meal for us that day and man, when you had a meal at Lorna's, you had a farm meal and you couldn't move when you finished.

Lorna wanted to know everything, how Daniel's year had been, how on earth he landed up in the Air Force, the condition of his new car, Daniel's girlfriend Bobbie. I knew a little about Bobbie and Lorna wanted to know about me since she had last seen me, everything I had done in the preceding year and a half. Daniel and I couldn't get a word in edgewise and we were quite tired from driving three days straight. We slept the rest of the day.

Next day, Daniel drove me down to his old Navy base Esquimalt on the island. There were his old commanding officers and personnel he still knew on the base. So Daniel introduced me to them. Next Daniel drove me around the greater part of the island with his nephew to see the First Nations communities and we got talking to them about traditions, the way they kept their communities alive.

The forestry had also resurged and there was a new lease of life in the business community as a year or so previously, the artists had done their job well with all the amazing paintings on different buildings. This helped brought tourism back to life on the island which led to openings and trade with the native community as well.

The capital of Vancouver Island is Victoria on the southern tip and is predominantly English with grand hotels and English gardens.

The contrast of North and South of the island is a little different. National parks are magnificent too. We did get to Nanaimo as well. Daniel had friends up there, including some military personnel.

The Butchart Gardens are a tourist attraction. You got to see this. It's a group of floral display gardens. These gardens receive over a million visitors a year so I am told and it has been made into a National Historic site.

There was lots to do in the weeks we were there. We took Daniel's nephew with us on our movements around Victoria. We stayed two weeks and returned via the car ferry to mainland British Colombia (Vancouver). Driving out of Vancouver that day was fine, just a little cold, and prior to reaching the Kamloops, we stopped at a rest area for a quick bite.

You won't believe what happened next. I drove off without my driving glasses and didn't realise. As I was driving, something wasn't quite right when I remembered raising my hand to the top of my head to find no glasses. We must have driven around 50 km before we had to turn back to go back to the rest area. My glasses were there on the table.

As I pulled out of the rest area, for some reason, I started to drive on the left side of the road as we do in New Zealand. I had driven over 3000 km and had a mental slip. I hit a Mercedes full of lawyers on their way to a business meeting in Vancouver, the wrong people to hit, and thought they had gone over the cliff. I could not see them at all in the rearview mirror. Daniel sat there laughing at my mistake and I had to tell him it wasn't funny. Fortunately I only had just knocked them off the road out of sight. These fellas were irate and the Canadian Mounted Police were called in. The officers went and got their side of the story and then came and got our side of the story. He just said to me, "I can do one of two things, I can throw you in jail for reckless driving or give you a fine." He proceeded to tell me that there was too much paper work to place a foreigner in jail so he gave me a fine. FORTUNATELY HE WAS NOT A FRENCHMEN OR ELSE I WOULD BE IN JAIL. The lawyers of course wanted to press charges but I think gave up since I was a foreign national.

The damage done to the Oldsmobile included a very bent side panel, a broken headlight, and a bent bonnet. We drove all the way back to Barrie like that, 4000 km. We drove this time all on the Canadian side of the border across the long prairies around Thunder Bay and into Barrie, Ontario in three days.

The car went to the panel shop under insurance for repairs. This panel shop had placed second hand parts and sprayed the panels on Daniel's brand new car. Somehow Daniel found out about this and told them in no uncertain terms to strip the panels and install everything new as it was under insurance.

My old friend Daniel could be stern when someone tried to take advantage of him. That was funny just watching him in this frame of mind not shouting but standing his ground. GOOD ON YOU, DANIEL.

Back in Barrie, one of the fellas that was associated with the Salvation Army in Toronto was a captain with Air Canada. Merv flew the Toronto to Heathrow England flights on Airbuses and was on days off when I met him. He was a very keen brass band player as well as an aviator like myself but Merv, having been a Canadian Air Force pilot and having years of experience as a captain, had just a little more experience in the air than me. Merv and his wife Peg were great Christian people who introduced me to all their friends, family, and extended family, and yes, there was a lot of them. In North America, going out for meals was easier and more convenient that staying home and cooking for yourselves, especially if it was a group. And that we did.

How I met up with Merv was playing my cornet in the Eaton shopping mall in Barrie, standing the kettles for the Salvation Army. Merv heard me playing and came right up to me and we got to chatting.

I'll never forget the wonderful comradeship of all the people that Christmas in the two-month break in Canada. I kept in contact with Merv and Peg. I know Merv was asked before he retired a few years ago if he would instruct on airbuses in Toulouse, France. Not sure if he accepted the contract as he would have had to live off shore. Peg was a lovely lady too, very warm and reassuring, very easy to talk to.

Like being with Burt and Marion, Merv and Peg were people that you could always come and see. The door was always open.

Within a week of being back in Barrie, Daniel lent me the Oldsmobile to go down and see some friends I had met in New Zealand who lived in Chicago. I had never driven there, let alone driving on a six-lane freeway with no GPS, just a map. Daniel said to me as a joke that day, "If you have another accident, don't come back," and had a laugh. Daniel also told me places along the way not to stop at or else your car would get stripped. I heeded his advice and didn't stop except for fuel.

Now Chicago was an eight-hour trip from Toronto and there was fresh snow along parts of the freeway. Arriving in a Chicago at 5 pm on a Friday night, I got stuck in peak traffic. Didn't know exactly where I was but I had driven to the South of Chicago and the directions that been given to me were not far off my destination, according to my map. Had an angel with me for sure.

A kiwi boy in unfamiliar territory.

Never seems to faze me that everywhere I travel, most people are willing to help if you have a problem. So panicking was never an option.

Arriving at Rick and Jean's place about 7.30 pm in suburban Chicago was another interesting part of my journey. Rick and Jean were waiting and were very pleased to see me. We had a bit of catching up to do on the events of the past year and a half and we had some sights to see in the next three days.

Rick drove me to downtown Chicago next day. Chicago is situated next to Lake Michigan, which is one of the five Great Lakes of North America. Parts of it ice up in the winter and storms prevail across these lakes throughout the year. These lakes are huge and actual ships and ferries cross them. The storms at times over the

THE NEXT ADVENTURE WAS STARTING TO UNFOLD

years have been so severe that ships have actually sunk.

Well, in Chicago, this is the city that Al Capone led his reign of terror in the late 1920s and early 1930s in the Prohibition years. So we did some historical research on Chicago and the city is well known also for its architecture, museums, its jazz music and foods, especially pizza, and of course as mentioned above for its 1920s gangsters.

We went up the Sears Tower 130 levels in a matter of seconds. Not sure if it was higher than the twin towers. Some of these buildings then were the tallest in the world when they were built but not now.

Rick, Jean and I just kept tripping around in the city of a Chicago and outer Chicago for the next three days eating and travelling by subway. It was snowing in between times and there was ice on the roads.

Rick also introduced me to his father who told me an interesting story. I will call him Bob. Bob was an Army Vet from WW2 and was in the D Day landing over Normandy, France. He was parachuting over Normandy and was one of the soldiers who was shot out of the sky by German machine gunners when near the ground. He was badly injured but survived. Bob showed me the scars where the bullets went straight through his lower abdomen. Bob survived and made a full recovery. Forty-two years on, he had lived a normal life and lived to tell the tale where there were others who weren't so fortunate. The war cemeteries of Europe are full of those who gave their lives for the price of FREEDOM. LEST WE FORGET.

Before leaving Chicago, Rick asked if I would be keen to come back sometime and travel with him up to Alaska and journey into the wilderness, as he too was a keen outdoors person. I made the comment that I would would love the opportunity. Thirty years later, I still would like to go back and do this trek.

Leaving Chicago later on the following Friday and travelling late at night on the freeway, I crossed the American Canadian border and hit a white out. The cloud base was complete at zero feet and the ice on the road was pretty bad. Slowing down, I went to take an off ramp and did a 360-degree spin on the freeway, worried my car would be hit both ways. Fortunately the traffic came in spasms, there would be a lot of traffic and then there would be a break. My heart was pounding as I got the break between traffic. I couldn't get to the exit and off the freeway quick enough. I got off and stopped at the bottom of the exit, closed my eyes, and was reminded of God's promise that he would send his angels to protect you. That had been my prayer before starting on this journey and was my prayer until I finished it. The song that came to mind was I'M IN HIS HANDS. WHAT EVER THE FUTURE HOLDS, I'M IN HIS HANDS.

I am not sure but the next morning there may have accidents on that freeway at that same point and the road had been closed. Two hours later, I was back in Barrie, Ontario. I never ever told Daniel about coming back and nearly writing off his Oldsmobile.

There was one more drive I had promised to make for a friend in Gisborne, New Zealand. Bess had a penpal in Kitchener, Ontario whom she had written to for over thirty years. Bess asked me if it would be possible to go and see her. Well, Daniel was back on base and the Oldsmobile went for a drive down to Kitchener, 166 km roughly and one hour forty minutes to find it was a Twin City Waterloo-Kitchener with the halfway mark in the center of town. This means you could be working, driving, and living on both sides of two different towns. Anyways, I got to see and stay with Mary, Bess's friend and went out for dinner that night. She was little old lady that was overjoyed to see me come on behalf of her friend in New Zealand.

At the same time, her son knew my profession as an electrician and asked me if I would be interested in working on a nuclear power station on this side of the Great Lakes as a job had been advertised by his company. It meant travelling back to New Zealand as planned anyway and applying through the Canadian Immigration. Lisa would have loved that. It was only a few days before I would be leaving the Canadian frontier for Los Angeles to see Rob on my way home. I did apply all those years ago for residency but got turned down by the Canadian government since I wasn't a refugee. What they really meant was that I was not bringing enough money into the country.

Two days later, Daniel drove me through to Pierce International Airport in Toronto, reluctantly said goodbye, and said he would travel back over the Pacific to see us when he could. Just before leaving, Daniel had got a posting to Bermuda for two years and it would be another year before we would catch up.

Leaving Canada and Flying to Los Angeles

I had been in contact with Rob in Los Angeles. He had been waiting to come and pick me up as he wanted to spend some time with me before leaving once again for New Zealand. Rob had actually set me up with his old girlfriend Vicky for a few days as he been called out for some business activities. Rob had completed his business management studies at UCLA and later walked me around the whole campus. Will get back to that later.

Vicky enjoyed taking me around LA. She also had completed a degree at UCLA and had gained employment initially with Lockheed Martin, an aircraft factory. Vicky actually drove me to one entrance built into the side of a hill, showing me how sensitive and top secret military contractors are to the government contracts. Vicky would have had a full background check and screening just to get past the front gate, without authorisation to enter other parts of the factory.

In her holidays, to raise money for her studies, she worked at Disneyland in Anaheim. This was great as she knew most of the staff and signed me in free. Last time when going into Disneyland with Rob, we paid $100 and had a stamp on our hand for all the rides and that same time 1985 was the 25th anniversary of Disneyland so they had massive celebrations which lasted up to midnight the whole week.

Getting back to Vicky, we spent the day there with all her friends, on all the rides, as many as we could. It was great. Next day, Vicky drove out to Santa Monica Beach a second time and to a few other great surfing beaches, then round the coast up to an old monastery on the hill overlooking the coast. The Salvation Army had acquired the property for their training base for ministers.

I think Vicky didn't want to let me go either; we were having a great time, I guess you could say we were dating. I liked Vicky too. Sometimes I wonder now what would have been if I had been allowed to stay in Canada with Lisa or come back to the USA for Vicky and continue on where we left off. Both girls wanted me to come back and it was disappointing when it was difficult to return.

Rob had a few days off now and we left Los Angeles for San Diego, spending a night in accommodation right next to a brothel. The accommodation was given to us at no cost, which is why we stayed there and locked the door. All night we heard these women outside saying, "There's some nice young men gone inside there, shall we knock on the door?" We just kept the curtains closed as they had congregated around the door.

Next morning the ladies had all gone and the coast was clear. We drove across to Las Vegas, an all-day trip. We made Viva Las Vegas that night. Finding a hostel in the middle of the bright lights was not too hard. And Vegas lived up to its reputation of bright lights casinos. Everything is different during the day; I thought Vegas looked mundane.

However, Rob wanted to take me into the casinos and experience the night life. We had all these bunny girls around us and it wouldn't have been difficult to smack some unsuspecting bunny girl hostess on the bum quickly, side step, and let Rob get slapped on the face. I told Rob that afterworlds. He just smiled. You can certainly see how people can be enticed to gamble and lose so much money on pokies, cards, and spinning the wheels, as I like to call it. We spent the night going from casino to casino. There were some live shows on and some live performers too. We even walked down a street that was partially blocked off as they were filming a live movie. Cars were racing around the streets in a chase.

We spent three days around Las Vegas. Really, Las Vegas is a night city. (Didn't get to see Area 51 on our way back to LA. Only joking). Then we drove back to Los Angeles again, taking turns in driving. Rob and I drove around the outer parts of Los Angeles when we got back utilizing most of the freeways in his trusted Toyota Corolla. We walked around all the buildings of UCLA campus, Rob telling me about the various people who had donated money to pay for each building. Rob also told me the cost for his tuition each semester was around $5000 and that was 1987.

Having reached the end my journey two days later, I was reluctant to say goodbye to Vicky, just giving her a big hug and holding on to her for a bit.

Once again, Rob dropped me off at LA International. There we said our goodbyes and I flew on a late flight, stopping at Honolulu on the way back to Auckland, New Zealand. I arrived back in New Zealand early March 1987.

WELLINGTON, NEW ZEALAND

My New Home for Two Years

Arriving back in New Zealand in early March 1987 gave me some time to rest and reevaluate how I could keep working towards my goals. My brother and his wife were leaving to work and travel overseas and the Wellington South Salvation Army band were preparing for a tour of Australia's east coast. Andrew had being playing in the band and he was leaving New Zealand. I was asked or should I say I asked to be a substitute player for Andrew, knowing they would be short of players on this mission tour. Got a phone call to come and play in the cornet section and attend all the band's rehearsals very quickly.

Immediately packing up everything including a bed and all my belongings, I drove down to Wellington, this time in my rebuilt Mazda utility. It could carry a lot of gear, including all my work tools and boxes. So that was me, I drove down with everything I had.

WELLINGTON, NEW ZEALAND

Initially I stayed with my aunt and uncle for a couple weeks till I found accommodation. In that time, I also found work on one of the many building sites high rise buildings as an electrician. There had been a building boom on in the late 1980s and work wasn't hard to find. Actually, I walked in from off the street to a company advertising for commercial electricians.

Within two weeks, I was renting an old two-story building near Victoria University with another fella who was a trainee bank manager. It wasn't the greatest of places to rent as it was damp, being in a valley, and a little cold in the winter.

With my job and reasonable rent now, I was able to complete my commercial pilot training at Wellington Aeroclub. Wellington Aeroclub was situated on the southern side of Wellington Airport, away from all the commercial airlines, but we still had to use the main runway for takeoff and landings, sometimes taking off before B737 or B747 and other heavy traffic. This built up some great experience in flight safety as well because there are very big jet vortices when a jet takes off or is landing. Taking off too close can actually flip an aircraft, especially light aircraft. Usually the controller positioned you within a three-minute delay before lining up or approaching to land. At both ends of the runway, there was water. Lyle Bay was on the northern end of the runway and Evans Bay on the southern end. So if a plane went off either end, it would land in the water. Fortunately those accidents are very rare.

I would make my way very early in the mornings before work for flight training and then race to beat the traffic to work. Or in the afternoons after work, I would go for an hour and on weekends.

At the same time, I was attending band practices twice a week at night, working as much overtime as I could and dating a girl. I tried to have those priorities in order.

One building site we were on, we had one fire on level five. The boiler maker had left a heater on in his workshop all weekend and over that weekend, the floor was burnt out. We had to rewire the floor again. Not long after that, a laborer threw a cigarette butt into the waste paper basket and the floor was incinerated once again. So the floor had to be rewired again. We did get to watch the 1987 Rugby World Cup with the New Zealand All Blacks winning the first ever title in England on a big screen on that floor after it had been refurbished. I think it might have been against Australia. The building did eventually get finished but there were some more funny stories to follow working on it, which I will explain.

As the floors were being finished, most trades were relocating their workshops and lunch rooms downstairs to the car parks that had been finished and no car parks had been allocated. Our company vans had been utilizing these car parks for work engagements. The custodian of the whole premises, remembering that stage one and two had been finished and allocated and we were working on stage three which was not finished, decided to place these hard-to-get-off stickers on our van. These stickers suggested we were parking here without authorization. At first we didn't take any notice of them as we thought no tow truck could get down the ramp to remove vehicles as the concrete ceiling was too low. Then one day we came down for lunch and saw the company van being towed away by a low level Holden one ton truck. At that point, all of us had to pay out $200 between us to get it released and tell our company management what happened. Management was appalled. A month or so later a West pac helicopter with police in it were tracking a runaway criminal just out of Wellington. The helicopter flew into the main feeder power lines, killing everyone on board and taking out the power in downtown Wellington. Banks closed up, emergency generators came on everywhere, and in our building, everything stopped. People were stuck in elevators, you had little men in their safety hats running around looking as they were trying to organise people who were taking no notice. We just stood and watched.

When not at work, I was flying as much as I could, practicing steep turns, maximum rate turns, simulated forced landings, simulated engine failures, basic stalling, stalling in the turn, instrument flying, low level flying, cross country flying between North and South

Island, loading and weight and balance checks. All these exercises had to be within +-5% to be evaluated by a government flight testing officer. So you can see a lot of work was involved mentally.

With all this happening and band rehearsals, my trusty Mazda utility was stolen in broad daylight in downtown Wellington. It had my aircraft log book inside, which was of no value to anyone else except me, my passport in my briefcase and a few other important items.

So I had no transport. My flight log book was gone, which I needed to verify all my flying hours for flight test. I think that was the hardest because I had to contact every instructor that I had ever flown with to verify all my hours and aircraft type ratings. Because I lived in the city, it was a hike but still I could get to the airport until another vehicle was sourced.

The work van picked me up and my girlfriend at the time, Valery, had a vehicle. She helped out a little. One time I went flying early Sunday morning and a sea fog rolled over Wellington Airport and couldn't land. I circled and circled until I was given a clearing and I was able to get under the fog, otherwise I would have had to fly to another airport on the coast. Dave and Kim were working at the control centre at Wellington Airport. Dave was in the Radar unit and Kim was in the tower.

It was around this time, the end of August or early September 1987, the Wellington South Salvation Army band went on tour to the east coast of Australia. We left Wellington and landed in Brisbane. This is where I did the first concert at the Brisbane Temple Salvation Army Church on Saturday night and led the church service on Sunday morning. Next day, which was a Monday, we bused up to Toowoomba via the Australia zoo as an excursion. We played with a few native birds on our heads, my cousin annoyed a sleeping crock with sticks, which got demolished, we saw a number of animals and then we bused on to Toowoomba. All I remember about Toowoomba is that it was very cold in the morning at that time of the year. The concerts were made up of band marches, classical

pieces, men's singing groups for gospel songs, some fun stage music, brass band solos and of course vocalists. We changed the music at each venue around as we had quite a repertoire of music. From Toowoomba, we went to Maryborough; from Maryborough to Rockhampton; from Rockhampton to Grafton; and from Grafton back to Brisbane. Each place we went to, all of us were billeted with some wonderful families. We had one day at Dream World and then flew back to Wellington next day. Some of the guys stayed on for a few days extra at Noosa. All in all, our thirty-five piece band did very well as we are a Christian organization which shares the gospel through music, word and action.

I was back at work on site the following day. Back to where I had left off. There were two other towers we were asked to work on as well. They had been building from ground up on one tower and had started building another level, I think it was the third level to the fourth. The construction engineers had started building on green concrete. You know what's going to happen. Yes the third floor collapsed and debris went flying. Fortunately, no one was killed. We did finish all three towers.

In that time in Wellington, I had another friend who was killed flying one night on an ambulance flight from Masterton, New Zealand (which is just over the mountains from Wellington to the north) to Wellington in a twin engine Piper Aztec. Phill got distracted with a mechanical fault on an instrument approach and flew into Mt Mathews, killing everyone on board. Emergency services were alerted immediately as the plane disappeared off radar.

This wouldn't be the first accident with friends killed in the commercial airlines.

People who knew Phill were on duty in the radar room and in Wellington tower that night, they were pretty emotional. Two controllers even walked off the job.

So you can see. life was very eventful in those years. The aviation industry is a small community and most of us have connections with aircrew and organizations involved around aviation.

This was also at a time I shifted into Dave's place in Karori, a western suburb of Wellington. Dave's place was a two-storied place in the valley that his older brother had built in recent months as a spec house. I would stay and rent a room till Vijaya and I got married.

Through these events, I was able to keep my composure for working through the day in the fast pace of the city life and flying every opportunity. Some of my flying was through mountain passes at low level at the top of the South Island of New Zealand; some of the other training was across in the Wairapa or Masterton side; and some training was on the northern side away from Wellington air traffic. By the end of 1987, I was ready to do my flight test and a testing officer was booked. Just before I did the flight test, my instructor and I were practicing some low flying. By the way the idea of low flying is if the cloud base gets too low, you need to able to fly and navigate at a certain height safely to land. This occurs with instrument flying and making an approach not below a certain height above sea level, otherwise a missed approach is commenced and an alternate aerodrome is required. Adrian the instructor and I were flying at low levels across Lake Onoke in the Southern Wiarapa at 400 feet. Now Lake Onoke backs onto the shore line of the Wairapa coast north of Wellington. This day, a man was laying on the beach starkers. Adrian said, "Watch this." We rattled across this fella at 400 feet. He got such a surprise and jumped up with everything hanging out. It was so funny. We flew from there straight back to Wellington. The fella had the chance to write down the aircraft's registration. Now back to the flight testing, there would be ground work as part of the test. The testing officer would be quizzing me on aircraft performance on type, weight, and balance, flight manual's aviation law, responsibilities as a commercial pilot, carrying passengers, commercial pilot's limitations and number of hours he or she could be rostered on flying duty hours and schedule charters. Then came the flying. I have to tell you, the first time with the testing officer, I failed on the paper work as I was quite nervous. However as it was the end of that year, in good will, Mr Testing Officer held the flight test over till end of January the following year. This gave me a clear path to have a clear mind and go straight into the flight test. This I did with another testing officer and passed. The plane I was using was a Pa 28, otherwise known as a Piper Tomahawk, a two-seater trainer.

What sealed my pass was setting up a simulated forced landing from 3000 feet into a paddock. I misjudged when establishing the boundaries from 1500 feet, descending to 1000 feet with no power, turning to high when descending down to final approach into the field. However, the field just beyond set me right up well to the descending 200 feet and at that point, I applied power to climb out and, using a pilot's term, make a go around. Mr Flight Testing Officer wasn't to know that and with all the other manoeuvres, keeping with +-5% accuracy, I passed.

We flew back to Wellington Airport and made a perfect landing.

Commercial Flight Test Passed January 1988

It was at this point I met a lovely young lady who happened to be my sister Fiona's friend. She has now been my wife and mother of my lovely children Rachel and Cilla for the last thirty-one years. Vijaya, my lovely lady's name, is of Fijian Indian descent. She had come to New Zealand with her foster parents Dean and Coleen Myers and their three girls in the mid-1980s from Fiji.

Vijaya caught my attention by not only her good looks but her Indian cooking, you could smell a curry a mile away, and of course her kindness. I would take her with me flying around New Zealand. My father and other sister Marie drove to Wellington from Gisborne for me to fly them both to Christchurch this particular week. Fiona's car was to be driven back north, driven onto the inter-island ferry, and driven off at Wellington.

Well, having checked the weather that morning, with coastal fog on the Kiakoura coast, the east coast of the South Island of New Zealand was clearing, I made the decision to plan the flight from Wellington to Christchurch at 2100 UTC the day before (or in laymen's terms, at 0900 am that morning). It was early October 1988 on a Thursday. Vijaya had taken the day off work to fill the last seat up in the Piper Cherokee 180 with my sister Marie and father Robert and myself. We flew out of Wellington across the Cook Strait (the water which separates the North Island from the South Island of New Zealand) and would have been airborne about an hour into flight when we hit severe coastal fog down the Kiakoura coast. Obviously, it hadn't cleared completely so we circled over the water off shore of the coast three times to see if we could get under safely or around it but it was no go. I remember Marie had never had a good stomach for travelling. She suffered from motion sickness and was just hanging on. At this point, I made a decision to use Blenheim Airport as an alternate. Blenheim is still in the South Island. Blenheim is a military airport open to civilian operations and situated inland from the Marlborough Sounds. The Marlborough Sounds also is where the inter-island ferry travels and berths at Picton at the face of the sounds.

We landed and no sooner had I taxied off the taxiway onto the grass area, I shut the engine down, opened the hatch, and got everyone out. Marie threw up then lay on the ground for around half an hour till she recomposed herself. She got up and became normal again.

Dad and Marie made the decision to catch the bus from Blenheim to Christchurch, a four-hour trip, stay the night, and drive north to Picton the next day.

Vijaya and I waited a little to see them off and flew back to Wellington. Vijaya didn't say much after we landed back at Wellington Airport but I knew she enjoyed the day with me, having held my arm in the front seat next to me all the way home. Dad and Marie did get that little Datsun car across to Wellington.

During those early months of 1988, I was making several trips from Wellington to Christchurch. I was either flying charters with friends organised or organised freight runs with Field Air Freight on their DC 3 Dakota Aircraft. These freight runs would be from Wellington to Blenheim to Christchurch. The process would involve loading and winching freight pellets up the main part of the cabin and securing them. The old girl could carry quite a few tons without a blink. Eventually, the faithful old DC 3 aircraft would later be replaced by the Canadian built Convair aircraft based out of Auckland International Airport, flying at pressurised altitudes direct from Auckland to Christchurch, New Zealand on a daily basis.

WELLINGTON, NEW ZEALAND

Just to give you an idea or the history behind field air. There was a man by the name of Lawson Field who had set up a top dressing company for farmers on the east coast of the North Island, New Zealand. This was after WW2 though it might have been earlier. He proceeded with De Havilland Tiger Moth aircraft, a biplane like the one I flew in Air Force cadets, and then went on to purchasing old air transport aircraft such as the heavy Lockheed Lodestar twin radial engines, the formidable DC 3 Dakota WW2 transport aircraft (these DC 3 are seventy-five-year-old aircraft and still fly in many parts of the world, also with radial engines) and the De Havilland Beaver. The latter were primarily built for short field takeoffs carrying good payloads of fertilizer, were built also for the Canadian lakes as float planes. The fleet of single engine Beavers and the DC 3s were used right up until the mid 1980s, dropping fertilizer on farm properties. Eventually the Beavers were sold and put back on floats sent to Canada. The DC 3 fleet stayed in New Zealand and were refurbished internally; the instrumentation was upgraded in the cockpit so aircraft could fly all weathers on radio navigation. And of course the aircraft fleet were repainted with a new color scheme from white and yellow in the fertilizer colors to white with blue and red stripes down the side of the aircraft.

Over the last twenty-five years, the DC3 aircraft were replaced by the Canadian turbo prop Convair aircraft flying at pressurised altitudes, being a bigger aircraft, a lot faster, carrying more freight.

Going back to Mr Lawson Field, as a kid I actually met him for the purpose of inquiring about a job sweeping hangars at the Gisborne airport. I didn't get the job as there were no jobs going but I got to meet him in person.

Back in Wellington those years ago, I was able to fly from Wellington to Christchurch on Fridays and return to Wellington on Monday morning. What was interesting in that old girl the DC3, there was no autopilot so controls were a little heavy in the air. Flying in the right hand seat as copilot gave me experience in the two-pilot environment on air transport. I would never get to experience the real quality of multi-crew environment after this in New Zealand, although I did fly on freight runs as two crew on smaller twin engine aircraft. Later I would use the flying environment, flying aircraft for my own electrical contracts in remote areas of the east coast. I will talk about that a bit later.

We were on a freight run to Christchurch one Friday night and a senior captain they called FEARLESS said to me, "We are ahead of schedule, son, let's fly this old girl inside the Kiakoura coast alongside the southern alps of the South Island of New Zealand." The Southern Alps is the mountain spine that runs down the center of the South Island, usually the peaks are covered in snow all year round and they separate the east and west coast of the South Island. It was a great afternoon to do just that and I still arrived early into Christchurch Airport.

Mission Trip to Tonga

The other reason I was commuting down to Christchurch a lot during that time was my involvement in a Salvation Army brass ensemble that was practicing for a two-week evangelical tour to the island of Tonga. The Salvation Army was opening up a church in the capital of Tonga and we were invited to go and play in the prison, villages, hospital and for the King of Tonga. The King of Tonga was a very big man. His son now holds the kingdom together as his father

ARRIVING BACK IN KIWI LAND

passed on some years back. So whilst looking after my dear Vijaya, working, building up flying hours, practicing hard and attending practices for this group called New Direction, I still managed to balance life without feeling completely exhausted.

We as a group met up at Auckland Airport. Some flew in from Christchurch, I and a few others from Wellington. We stayed the night at the Salvation Army church facilities in Auckland and flew out to Tonga the next day.

This group was good. The lead trumpet player was hilarious. He made music up as he went and wouldn't always stick to the script, but it was always in balance in time. Carl was his name for the book and he was a bandsmen of the renowned New Zealand Army Band. I think they had problems containing him as well. But in saying that, he had a big heart and was very good.

The rest of the guys and girls were very professional and a pleasure to be around. They were all good musicians and played a variety of instruments – trumpets, trombones, acoustics, drums, and base guitar. Brett on the base guitar was the brother of Carl and a gentlemen. About ten or twelve years later, Brett passed away all of a sudden at a very young age.

So here I was playing with all twelve and our leaders, Len and Jenny Kinge, who were also Salvation Army ministers.

We had a great gospel singer with us as well who complimented every part of our concerts and outings, that was Ange. Many people of Tonga were touched by the ministry. As an island nation, the Tongan singing is out of this world.

In Tonga, we were accommodated in central apartments and the villages brought in banquet-style meals. These are big meals with root crop, pork, salads, breads of some sort, chicken. You always knew when you saw fewer pigs roaming the streets what tables they were sitting on.

Some of the village food gave us the Tongan belly and quite a few of the group got diarrhea only by chance. Eating bananas in abundance was usually a prevention. I did this without realizing this.

But the diarrhea incapacitated a few of the group for a few days.

Some of the other excursions we went on were the famous blow hole caves on the east side of the island, having some time on the coral reef where some of us got coral cuts, including me. These didn't heal without antibiotics as I found out later.

Len, the minister, was also a rugby union player and had represented his province in 1st division championships in Manawatu. This is the area that surrounds Palmerston North.

On one of the days off, he was asked to have some input into the Tongan national rugby team and even a few of us rugby fanatics joined in the session. You could say we trained with these solid men as well. I would not have liked to face them in a game as they were big solid men.

The last few days in Tonga were spent helping construct and clean out the new Salvation Army facilities on the island. All twelve of us did this and had one last meal in the main townships as the following morning we would fly back to Auckland and then from Auckland back to Wellington. This was July, still winter. So we came back from high temperatures to cold temperatures.

When we departed Auckland on the way to Tonga, I was asked to be the technician on site. This meant carrying hand tools in a shoulder bag. This was before they introduced heavy security at all airports before September 11, 2001. Now we can't carry any metal objects, screwdrivers, etc because it could be used as a weapon.

I was placing my tool bag into the overhead locker in the cabin and accidentally dropped my bag of tools on the lady in the seat in front. She gave a grunt and, feeling terrible, I apologised profusely. That was the only safety breach I could think of on the whole trip. Fortunately, she didn't suffer from concussion. That was the Tongan trip completed.

Back to Reality in Wellington

Back in Wellington, I had these coral cuts that would not heal. I remember walking around with one side of my long pants rolled up

ARRIVING BACK IN KIWI LAND

just below the knee to try and let the air dry my infections out, which is a little funny when looking back but I would soon realise would need to see a doctor to get some antibiotics. It then healed.

The company that I had worked for the last ten months left as there were management and staff issues. I signed up with another electrical contracting company that had maintenance work all over Wellington, New Zealand. I saved hard again to go back to a flying school, this time in the South Island to complete instrument rating theory course. It would be a three-week course with class room lectures in four subjects, including flight planning, law, instruments and Morse Code. Every navigational beacon was in Morse Code abbreviation at the airport of origin. Also at the same time I got engaged to my lovely Vijaya. So it was a race to finish my exams and pass and save for a wedding in early January 1989.

The next three months, I worked solidly, worked some private electrical work for friends as well. This would be wiring out sheds and buildings, even installing temporary cables for lighting and power in temporary offices and placing electrical control boxes for sewage treatment plants and working for an electrical company at the same time.

I was starting to get a bit weary by this time. By September 1988, I had paid for the instrument rating course at Nelson Aviation college situated at the top of the South Island. In three weeks, I had absorbed everything that could be absorbed, done every instrument flight plan I could do, completed instrument law, learnt all the instruments used for flying on to and tuning into navigational beacons, and learnt Morse code at eight letters a second. I had sat the four exams and passed. Again, you had two years to complete the practical. This would include around twenty to thirty hours of training, including instrument cross country flights, holding patterns over a designated beacon, approaches off the hold, missed approaches climbing back up into the holding pattern, DME arc approaches, alternates and a government flight test in a single engine aircraft—all to have the endorsement issued on your license. Then to complete a multi-engine endorsement, you had to do the same again except this time with simulated engine failures in flight on the approach and on the climb out, flying on one engine, all within the -+5% accuracy. I would complete this in Christchurch, New Zealand the following year.

Arriving back in Wellington, having completed the course, we were now saving toward our wedding. We planned to have it at Gisborne, the ceremony at the Salvation Army church and the reception in my parents' very big garden at 105 Stout St. A year before, my sister Fiona and her husband Hub had their wedding reception in the gardens as well.

The Wedding Planner

I said to Vijaya, *"You'll never find another me. Not sure if that's a good or bad thing but it's the truth."*

Finishing work in December, Vijaya and I packed everything up, filled a trailer and drove to Gisborne, a six hour drive from Wellington. Vijaya had only been to Gisborne twice with me. I know she was unsure as she moving away from all her friends and her family of course and she was starting a new journey with me. She had to find a new job in a new place, but Vijaya had graduated from Wellington Teachers' College with a diploma in early childhood education. Vijaya had passed with honors, having attended her graduation in the Wellington town hall. With Vijaya in childcare and I having offered to operate an electrical contracting business which my father had originally set up with his building contractor business, we thought we would give it a go in Gisborne. Also I had my flying contacts in Gisborne, which gave me the idea of the flying tradesperson.

We would spend Christmas with our folks and plan and get

everything ready for our January 7th wedding in 1989.

We were able to purchase a house at a reasonable price in Gisborne as we thought we might stay in the area for a time. That was all arranged prior to the wedding, so we had accommodation after Vijaya and I came back from our honeymoon.

I wanted my best man to be Daniel from Canada but unfortunately he had been posted to Bermuda, so he couldn't make it. Dave, my air traffic controller friend, stood in with my brother Andrew and family friend Josh. Vijaya had all her bridal party sorted. We had vintage cars for our bridal party ordered as well.

Vijaya and I picked fruits and arranged our own caterers. Our own venue was catered for and we had a chapel. Vijaya had picked the design of her dress to be made, I had all the suits and shoes organised, and we had planned the reception for the people on that special day.

The 7th of January came and the wedding went off to a good start at first till one of my aunties had a heart attack and they had to call an ambulance. Then a fire truck raced by with sirens blaring, then helicopters were flying overhead, and finally the town clock that was outside the old Salvation Army church chimed on the hour. We did get through the wedding service with all guests and relations present. As we drove out in our three vintage Model-T cars, one stopped at a set of traffic lights and I remember my brother had to get out and push start it.

The rest of the day went all right and the reception in the garden went well, with live music, professional violinists and other persons. It was a great day for all and everyone enjoyed it. A wedding takes a lot of work and planning and you don't know this untill you have planned one. But the effort Vijaya and I put into it was well worth it for all the guests that came.

Following on from the wedding, my best man got married a month later to his lovely wife and spent the next thirty years air traffic controlling in the Emirates at a place called Muscat.

My brother pursued a building construction business in

Wellington, New Zealand for a similar period of time. And my young family friend Josh became a lawyer with a firm in Wellington, New Zealand.

Funny how you lose track of people you knew during a part of your life. Apart from my brother Andrew, I have never caught up with Dave or Josh, maybe briefly in passing in all those years. Vijaya and I went for our honeymoon around the North Island for a couple of weeks, having great weather and great fun, and came back to our new home and settled in.

Living on the East Cost of the North Island

In those first two years, I promised Vijaya I would finish all my instrument training, Turbine ratings and airline transport exams. It would mean spending a little time away from home in between working my electrical contracts. Looking back on it, I am not sure if it was the right decision. Spending all my energies trying to pursue a career in aviation sometimes put a strain on my young wife at the time and when I was away, I really missed her.

Eventually I decided for a time to utilise my flying to incorporate with my business. This meant flying into remote cattle stations or landing on beaches up on the east coast with all my tools and equipment for the jobs in the area. Flying up to the remote areas, the farmers were thankful that the cost would be shared by all farms or communities thus I managed to build up a good clientele. Also I had work in Gisborne.

Vijaya did work as a preschool teacher for the first two years before she fell pregnant with Rachel, my eldest daughter. Everything was going great for those first two years and with all the hard work done, I managed to complete most of the aviation courses except two Airline Transport exams and from there it shattered me a bit as it seemed to take forever trying to pass them.

I had a wife and a new baby and I was trying to provide and spend as much time as I could with them. Also I tried to spend time away with Vijaya and Rachel.

ARRIVING BACK IN KIWI LAND

I did have some funny experiences on the coast though. I phoned the store up at Te Araroa on the east coast to make sure the strip was clear. I was advised it was and after being advised some person must have released some livestock on the airstrip as no sooner had I arrived overhead I had to cattle muster them off. I did this by flying up down and around the airstrip till I got them all off and could land safely.

Another time I flew up there and there was a rather large Ferris Wheel and carnival happening. The locals kind of forgot to advise me that there was something happening this day and I had to make a real short field landing across the top of the Ferris Wheel and also a concrete toilet block. I did land with a few meters to spare. It was pretty wild up there and a lot of the old respected Maori fellas were out of the famous 28th Maori Battalion C Company, a very famous unit of the Second World War. These men were farmers or retiring farmers, forestry workers. There are very few if any WW2 veterans left today. I had great respect for them and their families and they always looked forward for me to come stay, fix and repair anything electrically that needed repairing. Also I was asked to do repair work in the little township as well.

These fellas would always leave me a car out when needed. I am not saying they were registered or fully roadworthy, but it gave the plumber and electrical inspector some hilarious moments when they came up with me to do inspections or repairs.

I was with the electrical inspector one day and the old HQ Holden sedan was left out with the springs in the front seat gone so you were low riding all the way to the job. With the plumber, a Chrysler Valiant was left out with big fat wheels. These big fat tyres do not accommodate metal roads well and the car slid around corners of that metal road to the east cape. The plumber was driving and he thought it was hilarious.

One day, I was left a Subaru Ute with the floor partially removed; you could actually see the road you were driving on from inside the cab. These fellas on the coast were my friends and I was always welcome. Sometimes I would be supplied with a quarter of a beast, maybe a killed sheep or pig as a thank you. These would be packaged by a butcher and supply the family with a year's supply of meat in the freezer.

There was another time one of the farmers was wanting new homes for piglets. Thinking this was a great opportunity to bag one little porker—yes, it was live—and take home with me from the job. Arriving home that night, I opened the back door of the van. The porker jumped out of the back and ran down the back section we had. I went to try and corner it but the stupid thing ran as fast as it could up the driveway across the road and into the neighbours' section. The neighbour came out and the two of us tried to jump on it, missing it completely. The stupid thing ran out down the street and into town. We ran around the corner. A policeman stopped us and said, "If you are looking for a pig, it ran in that direction." Next thing we had to do was ring the council dog handlers and explain to them we had a runaway pig. Trying to stop laughing, they sent out the handlers and they traced it to a park across the river from us. The porker had swum across the river and taken off. Thinking that was the end of it, at 11 pm that night, an irate Maori fella knocks on my door and says, "Is that your pig? It's just run into my car." This pig was more trouble than it was worth.

This started on the Wednesday. On Sunday, this porker had swum back across the river and was sunning in the marshes at the bottom of the section. My dear Vijaya had to be walking down the back there and comes running back, shouting, "The pig has come back." I went down there and, seeing it there, rang Dad to come down with a cage. By this time, the neighbours on our side of the river had come out and Dad had brought the cage. He was on one side of the marshes and I on the other side, trying to corner this pig. Well, this pig started playing with us in the mud. We were jumping, diving in the mud, the neighbours were laughing their heads off and eventually this little porker swam back across the river and disappeared. Meanwhile Dad and I were covered in mud, the neighbours in fits

ARRIVING BACK IN KIWI LAND

of laughter. This little pig ran away. It wasn't long after the porker swam across the river that a shot was fired and someone had a pig for their freezer. MORE TROUBLE THAN WHAT IT WAS WORTH. That was a story in itself but going back to those older generation of lovely Maori people, it's sad to say many of the old fellas and wives have passed on and even some families have moved from the area. But these were good years, years of developing my character and learning from those who had been through some hard times.

Working on Maori Maraes was a privilege. These people had real values and standards to be admired. I HAD A DREAM and these were some of the building blocks to my dreams. I didn't say focusing on my dreams would be easy, as a matter of fact it was extremely difficult and sometimes painful as I will show you throughout this journey. But God put this dream and a few others on my heart and as long as I have a heartbeat, I will pursue it.

These men and woman, young and old, I have had the privilege to work with and I will say these dream builders not dream stealers (which there are many) gave me inspiration in those difficult times and helped me claim God's promises in his word to receive. For in the book of James in the Bible, James says, "YOU DO NOT RECEIVE BECAUSE YOU DO NOT ASK." That means you must ask and without fear, our great God will always answer. He made the heavens and the earth in six days, will he not hear you asking to pursue the dream he has placed on your heart? Will he not place the right people along your journey if you ask?

In experiencing another part to my DREAM, I had previously talked about a Dehavilland Tiger Moth I became an owner of.

I had a contract to rewire these state houses and one of these houses was occupied by a fella Biggles. Not his real name. Anyway Biggles was the owner of the Tiger Moth bi-plane which he had sitting in a shed on the other side of the Gisborne airport, as he had been wanting to sell it. Seeing the pictures of SNAFU, the name he given to the plane on the wall in his living room, I asked if he still had his Tiger.

Well, you should have seen his ears prick up and he immediately asked me, "DO YOU WANT TO BUY IT?"

For the next two weeks after that every night he would ring me and ask, "DO YOU WANT TO BUY THE TIGER? I HAVE OVERSEAS BUYERS WAITING FOR EXCHANGE RATES TO BE MORE FAVOURABLE TO THEM."

Well, I caved in and put a deposit on it with my credit card. The bank wasn't too happy about that, but I secured the plane on trust.

Next thing I did was go and inspect SNAFU with an engineer, and what happened next nearly did backward flips. The bottom and top left hand wing had failed the fabric test. Yes, the wings are fabric over wooden ribs and strong. That means they would have to be unbolted and taken away to be, as they say in aircraft terms, re-doped by the vintage aircraft engineers. This plane had a history. It was built in Hatfield, England as an R.A.F trainer. During WW2, it was sold and brought out to New Zealand as a crop duster. It was pranged and rebuilt. So the wings had previously been refurbished with an American compound but the company had gone out of business.

The fellas drove all the way up from Hastings, a small city south of Gisborne, and trailed the wings back to Hastings and we towed the fuselage behind Dad's one tonne Ute to the Airport engineers' hangar via the back roads.

In two weeks, the wings had been refurbished and brought back. A bill was presented to me of $13,000 and it had to be paid within a week.

I wasn't in a position to pay out within a week so I immediately went to a group of aircraft enthusiasts and pilots who were rebuilding an old Lockheed Lodestar in a hangar at the Gisborne airport. I asked all of them if they would be interested in placing this vintage aircraft in a syndicate, that would keep the aircraft flying in the area and open to the public. Initially, they said no as all the monies were

ARRIVING BACK IN KIWI LAND

tied up in the hangar project with their own aircraft. Then came the phone call, we could advertise shares over the radio and local network. Within two weeks, we raised $85,000. I kept my share of $5000 for nearly twenty years and the bill for the refurbishment of the wings was paid off. The public enjoyed the flights from barrel rolls, loops, spins in an open cockpit environment.

The old girl had two funny traits. Because fuel is gravity-fed from a tank on the top wing to the gypsy engine, when you do a loop, you have dive to build up speed and you pull back on the stick and go over the top. The engine stops till you come out of the loop and the airflow strikes the prop and the engine starts up again.

The other funny thing is if you get a very strong headwind, cars on the ground can pass you and the aircraft seems stationary.

These first five years for us on the east coast of the North Island were building years.

Within three years of the birth of Rachel, we had another beautiful daughter Priscilla and she was my little queen who grew up to be as outgoing as myself and strong willed. Rachel is reserved and Vijaya is a loving but firm mother.

My parents didn't live too far away so, as grandparents do, they were always on call if help was needed. My two girls loved the times they spent with my mum and dad.

Many times in those years, I was able to take my daughters to work with me in a safe environment and they were able to keep themselves occupied in making and building stuff out of materials around them. We would also take them to my sister's farm in Tauranga, a few hours north of Gisborne, so they would meet up with their cousins who were of a similar age. Farms are always good because of animals such as cows, dogs, chickens, cats, riding behind tractors, getting muddy.

This would become the lovely years before the storm.

The events that were to come were unbelievable and I would

hope it would never happen to any family.

I still really wanted to take my family and fly the skies of the world and this is where I will begin in the next chapter.

The Nigerian Federal Bank Contract

In the early months of 1995, I had made contact with a New Zealand friend from Wellington who was living in Nigeria at the time. I will call him Karl for the purpose of this book. My intentions were to fly offshore and I asked whether he knew of any one or organization that were looking for aircrew.

Karl was associated with a church and faxed me back with a person affiliated to the church congregation, a man who had spoken in the church and was a top government official. I will call this man Paul for the purpose of this book. Paul was the manager of the National Petroleum Corporation of Nigeria and was often travelling on business to London from Lagos, Nigeria.

Karl suggested I write to him with my request. To my surprise, I received a quick response back with a documented contract.

Nigeria at this time was under military rule and the corruption was extremely bad. This contract had nothing to do with flying but was a contract of an over-billing of oil. A group of three men—Paul, an accountant of the Federal bank of Nigeria named Dr Rashman, and the main person Dr Vince Otoji, the deputy director of the Federal bank—wanted an outside contractor. When I mean an outside contractor, I mean an offshore contractor to cover this over-billing with a so-called legitimate contract of electrical appliances and computers.

I phoned Paul immediately and suggested this was a scam, as I had heard of many Nigerian scams that have duped the unsuspecting persons of hundreds of thousands of dollars. Paul quickly pointed out to me that he was the Manager of the National Petroleum Corporation of Nigeria and if I was not interested, he would find another contractor.

This contract amounted to $25,000,000 USD and the contractors cut was $5,000,000. This was the contract from the Federal Bank of Nigeria.

I could not believe this so I went and saw my lawyer and showed her this contract. Valery was very skeptical and her advice was to be very careful what you do with this. I saw some fear in her eyes. I then showed this to my father. We sat down and debated what we should do.

We asked ourselves whether this was real, what was the real reason behind this, what was the legality of this contract and also felt we should act on good faith that Paul was a very respected chief of his village. Meanwhile, Paul had phoned back and asked us for a decision within the next two days. If we said yes, Paul was adamant that my passport should be sent to the Nigerian embassy in Sydney and I should fly to Lagos.

It was a difficult decision we had to make. Dad argued with Paul that he would go on behalf of myself as I had a young family and wife. In the end, both our passports went to Nigerian embassy in Sydney for entry visas into Nigeria. We would find out later both Dad's and my identities would be stolen because of sending our passports to the Nigerian embassy.

Every night, we received faxes from the federal bank, saying everything had been cleared and what we needed to do. Also as happens in many African countries today, every little action required some payment. Yes, a bribe.

Dad would fly to Lagos via London in June 1995. Rachel as a little girl flew to Auckland International Airport in our plane and we had a meal with Dad before he flew out.

I know my mother was very worried for Dad as five years before he had had a heart attack and recovered but was also on medication. Dad had also had a growth removed from his vocal chords

THE NIGERIAN FEDERAL BANK CONTRACT

in the last year.

Mum, myself, my wife Vijaya and a family friend were the only ones who knew that my dad Robert had flown to Nigeria to sign this contract.

Robert landed in Lagos that June morning at the Mohammed International Airport. He was in a long queue at immigration when a man came running down the aisle asking for Mr Robert Stewart, Mr Robert Stewart come with me. So Robert was taken out and passed through immigration, no questions asked. Don't forget, there was a military government in charge and the airport was laden with soldiers on and off the Concorde. Every white foreigner was suspicious to them because many expats had come with companies to extort the oil rich country.

Robert was placed in a car and told to lie down in the back seat to avoid any suspicion then driven straight to the federal bank to meet Dr. Vince, the deputy director of the bank, to sign these papers. Robert was placed in a small room with security wire around the windows. Because of the bribes, he was asked to take a gift for the director. I think it was something that represented New Zealand, a small artefact. However, Robert signed the papers, thinking that was that and he would make his way back to the airport. But that wasn't to be so. Dr. Vince had Robert driven to his estate out in the countryside through the slums and villages to this mansion.

Robert was surrounded by all these very tall black men. He was the only foreigner there. When Dr. Vince arrived, he immediately showed Robert the five chests of blacked out US $100 bills, $25,000,000 in total, taken out of circulation of the federal bank.

Part of the deal was for us as contractors to clean the notes to the original colour. This wasn't a problem as chemical compound needed was photography developing cleaner. This cleaned the notes perfectly. We had to supply the chemical for the five boxes. These weren't just boxes, they were chests. Dad rang that day giving us information and saying he would be on his way home the following day.

Robert couldn't get out of there quick enough and back on that plane home. I'm not sure if it was the first or the second time out of Lagos airport when, running to the gate, Robert tripped and gashed himself. He flew back through London to Auckland, New Zealand and flight back to Gisborne. Four days away and travelling to the other side of the world and back, Robert was jet lagged and slept for a day or so. Meanwhile, the phone calls and faxes kept coming through the day and night. Nigeria has a big majority of Muslims and Dr. Vince was no exception; he was very powerful and dangerous as well. The most unusual thing he did was send a Bible to Robert and, hidden in the lining of the book, were cleaned $100 US bills, just to prove the chest's money was real.

We told no one about this. I remember Robert, Mum and I sat down, closed our eyes, and, you might feel a bit skeptical, but prayed, "Dear God, what should we do?"

Most people, without hearing the story, believed my dad was being greedy. That was not the case. Robert had given of himself selflessly and we asked the question what we could do to make something that unscrupulous people would do at the expense of others and turn it around for the good. This was the African underworld you were dealing with, as we didn't find out till two years later. Interpol was after this international syndicate and Robert would eventually lead them right to the main people.

Robert reluctantly went back to Lagos for the last time. The bank and Dr. Vince and his accountant wanted some more papers signed. This time Robert was locked in a small room, not knowing what was going to happen next.

There was a guardian angel looking after Robert, a young man very well-educated and the assistant to Dr. Vince. Abil Dowdi knew what was going on and after everything was signed secretly, he got Robert out to the airport and on the flight back to London then Auckland, New Zealand. None of these banking officials had known that Robert had left the premises.

Robert again had been away for another four days without anyone

THE NIGERIAN FEDERAL BANK CONTRACT

knowing. The only person wondering where Robert was the owner of the house Robert was building.

The phone calls kept coming. You would think we would have stopped any more interaction with these fellas but we still were enticed to fulfill this contract.

What these fellas Dr. Paul, Dr. Rasman and Dr. Vince asked Robert to do was to have documents signed at international banks in the Netherlands, Germany and the UK.

They themselves didn't want to be seen as foreign diplomats at these international banks. All they wanted to do was get these chests of US dollars out of the country. They were flying Robert all around the world through some very not-so-very friendly countries from South Africa to Pakistan then to London and Canada then Rome, paying Robert at the same time.

Also I must mention there were other dubious persons in Nigeria trying to cash in on this so-called contract as well. We would be receiving a host of other faxes as well.

In England, Robert had met the fella who would steal his identity to operate in South America without Dad knowing. Dad's full name was Robert James Campbell Stewart. This Englishman's name was Robert Hershel. I will explain what Robert Herschel did to steal Dad's identity shortly. He too was part of this syndicate.

When Robert, our Robert, found what these bank officials and oil corporation executives were doing, he called it quits. They were money laundering and possibly involved with other devious businesses, such as drugs. Robert my father was a man of integrity and morals. He wanted no part of a business that destroyed other people's lives with these wicked deeds. Remember Interpol were trying to track down this syndicate and eventually my wonderful father would lead them straight to them at some considerable cost to my himself, and Mother, and my siblings.

It was at this point Robert said he would not do any more deals, sign any more contracts or bank paper work. He was tired and wanted to go home.

These men from Nigeria didn't take too kindly to Robert removing himself from what they interpreted as their legal binding contract and they were angry. Nothing could be finalised as we were holding this contract up and they could not proceed further without removing Robert and myself from the deal.

What these men did next would nearly tear my family, siblings and so-called friends apart. Robert was flown to Peru on his way home to New Zealand, except he would never make it home for another two years.

Dr. Vince had arranged a meeting that was of no avail to pretend everything was in order and had his hench men swap Robert's personal bag, same color, same weight, with ten kilograms of cocaine.

Robert was eventually dropped off at the international airport in Peru without being aware of anything different about his bag.

Checking in, immediate alarm bells went off. Police and dogs surrounded Robert and he was asked if these were his bags. Not knowing anything different, Robert said yes.

Robert was then detained, stripped, humiliated, shackled and asked where these drugs had come from and what syndicate was sending out these bags of cocaine.

Robert was sixty-two years old, unsuspecting, and very upset to the point he fired back at those who were beating him, telling them to leave him alone. Robert was put in a holding cell with passport, money and travelling documents taken from him.

Mum and myself hadn't heard from Dad for a couple of days as he usually phones at some point.

That Dreaded Call from Foreign Affairs
Wellington, New Zealand

All men make mistakes, but a good man yields
when he knows his course is wrong and repairs the evil.
— SOPHOCLES —

THE NIGERIAN FEDERAL BANK CONTRACT

It was a Monday morning in June 2000. As you can see, this whole Nigerian plot went on for nearly five years and only Mum, Dad, my wife and I knew about this.

That Monday morning, we received the shock of our lives. I was at Mum and Dad's place when the phone rang. Answering it, the New Zealand foreign affairs were wanting to speak to a Mrs Stewart.

She listened and was advised Robert Stewart had been arrested in Peru on serious drug charges. I just saw my Mum, my courageous Mum, collapse and start sobbing. Of course the rest of my siblings would need to be told before the media would try and get ahold of the story.

The first reaction from my brother, brother in-law, and sisters was one of anger and tears. The question they kept asking was what Dad doing over there in the first place. Our dad would never have any involvement in drugs. Then the media tried to get hold of a story. Fortunately, my wonderful father-in-law, who was the president of the National Party of New Zealand, stepped in to be the spokesperson for the family and gave no information. The press just tried to make up a story as they do about a man from the Salvation Army arrested in Peru on serious drug charges.

My father-in-law Dean Myers made contact with Prison Ministries International Washington DC and they made contact with Prison Ministries Peru. Prison Ministries by the way was set up by Chuck Colson, the lawyer who went to jail for Richard Nixon after the 1974 impeachment trial. Chuck became a Christian and set up Prison Ministries International.

This wonderful lady called Elsa searched and searched till she found Robert being detained in a prison called Lurigancho Prison at the bottom of the Andes Mountain. Designed for 1500 inmates, the prison had 5000 inmates in this jail and I mean everything was paid for by the prisoners in this jail, including the cell.

This wonderful godly lady was the person who liaised between the prison commandant and our family. We as a family set up a trust to maintain Dad's ability to live, eat, communicate and also buy a cell for $500 US dollars. Imagine buying a cell for $500.

I have to give credit to Marie and Peter, my sister and her husband, who worked so hard under the circumstances to get Dad support as well as my brother Andrew and myself.

I remember Dad in tears on the phone, distraught and not knowing what to do. But out of this dreadful situation came some hope.

Dad's needs were all met and he received everything that was sent to Elsa in order to pay off the commandant with various small articles. It was just the way it worked in these countries. People are so poor, they do whatever it takes to survive. It was even worse for nationals in this prison. Dad said to see young fellas selling themselves to stay alive was horrible.

Even if you had a cell phone it could be confiscated by the guards and you would have to buy it back.

Robert did get very down for a while, feeling very alone in his cell. But Elsa kept visiting him every chance she could. The story took a turn as Robert took in around six South African inmates in his cell. One was an undercover cop. The other five were arrested trying to smuggle drugs back to South Africa and the last person was a pilot apprehended on drug smuggling into the USA. He later got out.

The undercover cop had enough information to topple the South African government; that was the reason they would not get him out. (The South African government was under President Mbeki.) His dear wife was also a cop and under all the stress had suffered a heart attack.

In this jail, you could just about do anything in the system, even ring out on international phone calls, by hooking up telephone cables and bypassing the prison network.

At this point, I had this crazy idea of using my friend's oceangoing boat which I had rewired to secretly sail over to Peru and get Robert out. Dad even wrote a fiction book about how you actually could escape through the linings of the walls to the outside of the prison.

The number of prisoners to the number of guards was

THE NIGERIAN FEDERAL BANK CONTRACT

disproportional.

The boat would have made it, but being sure Robert got out through what he saw as failing maintenance around the prison might have also caused him considerable stress.

In New Zealand, our so-called friends were condemning. People Robert didn't always get on with were more concerned about Robert's well being. This was a very stressful time for everyone in the family.

The New Zealand police had wiretapped my parents' phone as family and friends trying to reach Mum were intercepted by police. They were also trying to find charges to incriminate Robert but they had nothing to go on. There were rumors going around that drugs had been hidden inside the walls of Mum and Dad's house. This was completely inaccurate.

Now in this cell through some ingenuity, the phone was rigged up. With this cop sitting in Robert's cell with phone numbers for Interpol, Robert was able to make contact. Remember, Interpol cannot be contacted unless urgent information is needed and this information came from Robert's meticulous memory.

This becomes the most incredible part of the story. From a prison cell, Robert was able to step-by-step go through all his travel itineraries, places stopped, airlines flown, and, yes, the true footage of the Italian Police being bribed by Robert Herschel on account of Robert's identity at the Rome railway station.

At the same time, a South African *60 Minutes* assignment team had been through the prisons in South Africa, assessing the conditions, and had heard about some South Africans who had been arrested in Peru on drug charges. They were in this Prison Lurigancho and they were all in Robert's cell.

The woman from South Africa's 60 Minutes wanted to do a full interview inside Dad's cell. I still have the DVD. Robert had never wanted to see it. When he got out, that prison was a chapter of his life closed.

Meanwhile Elsa was working as hard as she could on the days

she could to visit Robert and his spirits began to lift up.

The attorney in the courts were trying to lay a conviction for drug smuggling of twenty-five years for Robert and Robert would not plead guilty to falsified charges. So the courts delayed proceedings. Meanwhile in New Zealand, the bills started to mount up and my parents had to eventually sell their home. Mum was helped to shift house and clean out all of Robert's essentials and other things he had accumulated over the years. Mum was quietly grieving, although she was a strong woman.

I even had a friend who was a police detective insisting we give them information. Everything we had on the last five years was collected and given to our lawyer very quickly and held in his safe. There was nothing that would incriminate Robert at all and we did not want information that the police were not entitled to get into the wrong hands.

Meanwhile we were able to communicate through phone calls and writing letters.

The scariest letter I got was that Dad wanted my signature. My immediate reaction was no as someone would forge it. His reply was that no one can actually forge your signature as you had certain pressure points that no one can accurately copy. Dad told me Interpol was going through my bank accounts where I worked and lived, my comings and goings, as I had $18,000,000 US clocked up on my passport. Someone had stolen my identity and Interpol knew I flew and was an electrician. Dad said if I was dragged over here to face any false criminal charges, he was worried I would not survive this jail.

Now what happens next? All these embassies, including Great Britain's and New Zealand, were all condemning. I will leave it there.

No information was ever released to the New Zealand press. Good thing, as I think about it now, it would have ended up fake news to get a fabricated story and this is the real reason I am writing these accounts, not to cover up anything Robert or I did but to tell a story and hope no one else would fall victim to

THE NIGERIAN FEDERAL BANK CONTRACT

unscrupulous people. There is no shame with any Church because people can hide behind Christianity but even true believing Christians are not perfect and as the Bible says, "WE ALL FALL SHORT OF THE GLORY OF GOD. BUT HIS FREE GIFT THROUGH OUR BELIEF AND FORGIVENESS IN JESUS IS ETERNAL LIFE."

I think passing judgement is not helpful for anyone. Sure, it changed the perspective on how my siblings saw Dad but forgiveness was the main concern of many other people.

Dad's interaction with Interpol was nailing crooked judges and drug cartels worldwide that were part of the Nigerian ring. Arrests were made in England, Canada, and South Africa, just to name a few countries. At the same time, the president of Peru, being half-Japanese, absconded from Peru to Japan with a considerable amount of money. The new president that came in was pardoning wrongfully convicted prisoners on remand. Dad believed and knew his name would eventually come up on that board. Everyone laughed. The British consulate, Prison Ministries and I even think the New Zealand government thought the same, that Robert would never get out except on medical or compassionate reasons. Elsa didn't and she believed in Robert and knew his faith in Jesus Christ would sustain him and he would get out.

Yes, Robert's name eventually did appear on that board to the disgust of those who were trying to lock a man up for some considerable years. I often think what if some of these fellas faced corruption charges as well?

Paul got caught up in something very hard to get out of. Paul was my age with a young family, a Chief, a man of honor. There were many times we spoke on the phone about our families and values that were important to us. But this was no excuse for him to go down the road he chose.

Robert Herschel was the first to arrive in South America for a conference. The police in Peru had been tipped off. He was initially arrested and held in custody but somehow managed to bribe his way out. He disappeared for a bit but was picked up in Chile and brought back to Peru to face charges.

The next to arrive was Paul. He was traveling as a government official. Paul pulled out a gun and shot a cop. The police fired back, not sure how badly hurt Paul was. Paul was detained by the police.

Then came the prize, Rashman and Otiji both on the same flight to Peru. They too were intercepted by police. Men who callously would take away another man's freedom for the sake of purposely lining their own pockets had the tables turned on them.

Whilst these men were away from their homes, Robert had told Interpol exactly where all this money was hidden and I think all these chests of stolen money from the federal bank of Nigeria, the money that belonged to the people of Nigeria, I would like think was returned.

Meanwhile Robert's release now was imminent. How ironic, whilst Robert was being released, these men would be going into the same prison to meet the same conditions as Robert had endured. To this day, I don't know if they have been released by their own government intervention or remain disgraced or paid their way out.

These men may have claimed immunity as government officials, but I dare say they were detained. I certainly believe they would be very angry men and would seek revenge if they could.

I think also, they would be a little confused how anyone would have known their comings and goings and were waiting to apprehend them.

Who was the snitch? Had they known Robert had been in this prison, surely they would have known? Had they known Robert had been released?

Released From Lurigancho Prison

Real heroes are men who fall and fall and are flawed, but win out in the end because they've stayed true to their ideals and beliefs and commitments.
— KEVIN COSTNER —

Robert was released in June 2002, walking out of the prison into Prison Ministries in Peru. These same people who had kept Robert alive through Elsa nearly fell out of their chairs.

Everyone asked, "What are you doing out of prison? How did you get out? It's impossible." Nothing is impossible for God, His timing is always perfect. Just like Peter in the Bible, the saints prayed for his release and when he was released and turned up in their house, they could not believe it.

So be careful what you pray for. God through Jesus has a habit of showing up.

Robert asked to have his passport returned and personal items returned as well. He was going home. He was boarding that plane he had missed nearly two years prior.

The emotional moments with the two years of care that Elsa gave to Robert and the staff that supported her would remain embedded in Robert's heart for the rest of his life. Having spoken to Mum just recently, Mum also reminded me of a nun that was also involved with Elsa in looking after Robert.

I am hoping to make contact with Elsa, hoping I can reflect on some of Dad's time spent with her. I want to thank her again for keeping my Dad's hopes of returning home alive. Also keeping Dad alive. Dad did keep in contact with Elsa for a number of years and he also learnt Spanish in that prison. When I think back, Dad had an incredible memory. I learnt his reading skills and to this day enjoy reading books, enjoy learning about history as he did, being creative.

I've seen my father cry and it's not a cowardly thing for a man to let your emotions out. But this would be a goodbye forever. Robert would never return to Peru.

My mother was told of Dad being released. I think the emotion of packing up house, temporarily moving into a smaller unit, leaving the area she had lived in for forty years and finally her husband coming home after being incarcerated for nearly two years, caused

Mum to cry. Robert had sketched a picture of my mother in that prison which was laminated and is now kept as a memory of those dark days when Robert thought of seeing Mum again and it gave him strength to know that he would.

A day later, Robert was on his last flight home. This would be his last flight ever out of New Zealand. The family quietly got my father into the country without any press, which was amazing. My sister, brother-in-law, Mum, my two girls, and Vijaya and I were all there to welcome him home at Auckland International.

It was a very emotional gathering and a quick moment to get Robert out of the airport.

Questions would remain to be asked by families and friends and Mum's phone was still being tapped by New Zealand police even at this stage. There was nothing to incriminate Robert and even with a full pardon from Peru he was still classed as a suspected criminal by the New Zealand police, which I thought was very unfair. There was no evidence. Robert only heard from Interpol once more and that was that he should not say anything about these men and their evil deeds as they could have henchmen come and take Robert out.

Robert did not hold any grievances towards these men; he had forgiven them for what they had done.

Mum and Dad had lost everything they had so worked hard to gain over a lifetime but they still had each other. Dad quietly got on with his life although underneath he felt a little inadequate as all his working life, he was able to manage his affairs through good times and bad times. But now he had limited resources. His age and his health had caught up to him. I will say this, Dad was no quitter. He wrote two books, re-modeled two houses, continued to provide housing inspections, rebuilt one sports car, and loved his brass band music. I was involved in a brass band he established and had many fine weekends playing with some of the best brass bandsmen in New Zealand. He visited sick people with Mum, collected for annual appeals, and visited family. Dad tried to be active as much as could despite medical problems due to age. Dad was quite stubborn and a proud man. Proud of his family and very thankful to his family.

My mother and father were together for 57 years before Dad passed away unexpectedly in late 2017. Dad in his life time had been a Queen Scout. He wrote to Queen Elizabeth in recent years and gave her details of events over the last 55 years since attaining his Queen Scout certificate signed by Elizabeth Royal. Dad received an acknowledged reply back. I keep this letter.

Dad had travelled the world as a young man, which was pretty unheard of in those days.

Dad met my mother, an English nurse on a ship going to Australia, and married her in England.

Dad was a master builder and in those years had been very successful.

Dad always provided for his family and helped me and my siblings where help was required.

There was the time when my sister and I were traveling out of town one Friday night. It had been raining hard and there had been slips and boulders falling. I remember being behind a cattle truck in Dad's Holden Ute as the cattle truck swerved to miss some heavy rock. I swerved but not enough, hit the rock completely, buckled the drive shaft and pushed the radiator into the fan blade. This was in the pouring rain and my sister and I had come to a complete stop. The only place we could see was a ranger station on top of the hill, so we ran up there in the rain to contact Dad. In the middle of the night, Dad drove to where we were and towed us all the way home. That morning, he was flying to Fiji as a volunteer builder to help a village be reconstructed securely after a major cyclone. That was Dad. Known to the Fijians as Bulla Bob. He was a man who cared about others. He was a family man, a good father, a good husband and even in the years my sister Fiona suffered from anorexia, Mum and Dad were still there for their grown offspring. Dad was a fun man as well. He loved a good joke.

Dad, I salute you and know I will see you again one day.

In the times leading up to Dad's incarceration, I had gone to Fiji in search of a first officer's job with Air Pacific, now Fiji Airways, as I was disillusioned with the electrical scene. Vijaya was still a Fijian national and I thought there was a good possibility of reaching the flight deck of a B737, which there was. The first time arriving in Fiji, my goal was to see management at both Sunflower Aviation and Air Pacific. Making the appointments on the spot did not seem hard at all as I had an interview with the online manager Air Pacific and also an interview with the chief pilot of Sunflower Aviation.

The online manager for Air Pac was a captain from Air New Zealand, an expat working with the Fijians. I cannot remember his name but we had a full discussion about my flying portfolio, the companies I had been associated with. Would I be willing to relocate? What are my expectations? John the airline manager also said to me, "You have to get something close to being a Fijian national and if you can get that, we would consider placing you on the next B737 course." At that time, I was elated but my problem was the Fijian national or citizenship.

THE NIGERIAN FEDERAL BANK CONTRACT

John the line manager had advised me that some other pilot had done the same as I had basically done, had actually got the position, and when the Fijian union found out about it, they were not happy. The fella kept his flight position but was not promoted very fast.

Now I had the dilemma of either Vijaya becoming a full Fijian national and renouncing her New Zealand citizenship, which would be crazy, or I would have to get a lawyer involved to help me through the legalities. This I did, a friend that was a Fijian Lawyer worked tirelessly. Three times we tried and three times the Fijians made it difficult for me. The second trip, Vijaya came with me to Air Pacific management and I travelled in my pilot's uniform to make myself look professional. This time management had changed within a space of six months and it was a Fijian online manager and she wasn't so accommodating. Again my hopes were dashed, but I moved on.

Fiji is a beautiful part of the world. The Fijians are generally happy smiling people and the Fijian Indians are hard-working business people.

The climate's great and living space is great. We as a family could have lived for a time as expats. The two main islands of Fiji are Vana Levu and Veta Levu and another 300 smaller islands that make up Fiji. We would visit a number of these islands in later years as a family or with friends.

So you can see with all these interactions and disappointments was the building up to leaving the east coast of the North Island for the Bay of Plenty, Tauranga area. It was another three years before we as a family would leave Gisborne for good.

The millennium came and went. People were believing the computer world was going to crash at the turn of the century. But it didn't. The east coast of North Island was the first to see the sun of the new millennium. Mt Hikurangi, the western side of Ruatoria, was the highest point to catch that first sunrise. I had flown past that mountain many times on the way to Te Araroa.

In the last five years before leaving Gisborne, in between my electrical contracts, I was flying some freight runs with a company called United Aviation. United Aviation was based out of Palmerston, North New Zealand. The routes would be Palmerston to Wairoa to Gisborne and back in the evening. Sometimes stopped into Napier on the way back. Some nights I would stay overnight and catch the next flight back. Then there was the night run, either Palmerston North to Wellington or Christchurch carrying Ansett freight. That's when Ansett was flying in New Zealand. I did this for a while and renewed my instrument ratings with the company on a BA57 Beach Baron.

It worked out well for some of the air crew as they would come and help me re-wire housing for Housing New Zealand when they had nothing to do during the day.

These young guys who I got to know were very good workers, as they had to be because they were on contract to United Aviation and they weren't paid a high salary. Most of these general aviation pilots were only there working to build their hours up and eventually jump ship to the airlines.

On these same projects with Housing New Zealand, I had a group of ex-military servicemen working as trade assistants for me, pulling cables. They came in a little later to help me finish off the contracts. They were elder men. Some had just finished active duty and some had been retired for a while. They were all a band of brothers and knew each other. Four in all.

Well, one of these fellas was George and he was a very capable. George had just finished in the military as a warrant officer and a very capable and loyal man. He was one of those disciplined Maori fellas that you didn't want to mess with. George did everything meticulously from digging trenches for cables to running cables. George had dug about three short trenches to run underground mains one day in a housing state area. That night these young fellas who had nothing better to do came and filled his trenches in. George arrived the next morning to find his trenches partially filled in.

The first thing George did was go home and get army combat

gear. Then he dragged these young fellas out to dig out his trenches. He knew who they were. If I had done that, I myself would have been given all sorts of derogatory comments. George was a very respected man. Matter of fact I think his whole family with the name Hokianga were well-respected.

I have to say, the other fellas were very well-respected as well.

Speaking to some of his relatives in later years, George was in his fifties and could not get a job in New Zealand, so went to Perth, Australia and worked as a security guard. Then he did two tours as a shotgun rider in Iraq with some Aussies, making $1500 US a day as a contractor. You never messed with George or you would come out second best. George later came back to Australia, worked up in the mines in Western Australia, and finally retired in New Zealand. Not long after that, he passed away.

So as you can see, I managed to run a business and fly air transport at the same time.

Getting back to flying with United Aviation Palmerston North.

One of the fellas I actually flew with on a number of trips a few weeks before had even been swimming with him down at a river inland from Palmerston. Tom was on an Ansett freight run from Palmerston North to Christchurch at night. He was flying a light twin Beach Baron B57 via east coast Wiarapa Radio Navigational Chart that night. A usual flight tracking on RNC (Radio Navigational Chart) Radials was via Wellington to Kai Koura to Christchurch.

This particular night, there had been heavy ice forecasted at certain levels along charted routes and Tom disappeared off Wellington radar. It was thought that the ice had glazed the leading edge of his wings and tail plane, causing a nose pitch up at lower airspeed and possible stall of wings or tail plane, followed by a loss of control before hitting the ground.

Investigations into the accident found that Tom went to sleep after carbon monoxide poisoning. This was probably due to a leak in the exhaust manifold system coming through the cabin heater, which would have been used on a cold night.

Tom was not fully aware or maybe he should have been aware, as carbon monoxide fumes actually give you headache initially and shuts off oxygen to the brain. Adequate cold fresh air would have illuminated the problem.

Tom died a young man. Investigations found severe maintenance problems. I will leave it at that. The company was under investigation by the New Zealand Civil Aviation and a few fellas and ladies lost their jobs.

Leaving the East Coast of New Zealand

If at first you don't succeed,
try doing it the way your wife told you.

By the end of the decade, which was the end of the century and a new millennium, I had become very disillusioned with my work and the flying environment. It just felt like the harder I worked, people around me just used me. I learnt who my real friends were.

When Dad was arrested in June 2000, this was the final event that caused me to close my business, sell up, and quietly leave Gisborne with my family. I had lived and worked there for nearly twelve years. Nobody said anything when we left.

From Gisborne to Auckland, New Zealand, initially I was working on a reconstruction site. It was a $280,000,000 sewage treatment plant upgrade in Mankau Auckland, and I had to fly home every two weeks. The project incorporated ultraviolet lighting that broke down raw sewage into natural water again. It actually was quite an interesting site. There were over a thousand personnel working on site. The electrical company I was working for was called Tyco. I ended up buying shares in this American company at $25 US a share. This was offered to employees of the company. The highlight of this was being sent the shareholders' manual and being asked to attend shareholders' meetings all over the world.

It was great till the company got hit by corporate fraud. The CEO and his accountant nearly broke the company. The shares dropped to $12 US but this was the best time to buy them as eventually they went back up to $32 US a share. Tyco was a parent company of many other companies, including electrical, electronics, and fuel systems, all of which made profit for them. Eventually I would sell shares and purchase a property in Tauranga.

It was good being able to stay with friends Dan and Julie in Papakura, South Auckland who were once again accommodating me. Sixteen years before, I had stayed with Dan and Julie when on my commercial pilot training course. In between times, I had also flown into Ardmore Airport with all my tools to wire out Dan's shed in Papakura.

I had flown around the country on many occasions prior to leaving Gisborne to do electrical work for clients and friends. These were small adventures for friends and clients. Clients who also became friends would always welcome me and family. Also they were there for us and I will always acknowledge those dear people.

If you find a true friend in life, you are fortunate. If you find more than two true friends in life, you are grateful.

The treatment plant was one of the first big electrical projects I had ever worked on and this really gave me a start into the heavy electrical engineering industry. They called us the POO CREW and we even had it embroidered into our company shirts. This project lasted for many months and as it progressed Vijaya, Rachel and Priscilla were in Tauranga or, as Captain Cook called the area, the Bay of Plenty. They were closer for me to come and go to work, leaving early each Monday morning and driving home to Tauranga on the weekends.

With the development of the UV lighting plant, UV meaning ultraviolet rays, they were eventually able to breach the big sediment pond walls near the Manukau Harbour as all sewage had been processed into natural water and the methane gas was burnt off through big flares over the sludge tanks.

When this project eventually finished, I was able to fill in with some contract work in Tauranga. And in Tauranga, I met up with my good friends Ronald and Jasmine.

Ronald had been an electrician and had bought into dairy farming initially. Having sold the farm when prices were high, he purchased a Kiwi fruit farm in a place just out of Tauranga, a place called Tepuke. Ronald told me at times when the market was not good, he would have to go back to being an electrician to subsidise his income. Farming of any kind has its good years and bad years. Eventually, Ronald was made an offer for the farm which he couldn't refuse. He sold and went into purchasing commercial property and aircraft. This is pretty much where my story begins with Ronald and his lovely wife Jasmine.

As I had mentioned before, Ronald was an electrician, I am an electrician; Ronald holds a Queen Scouts award like my dad had, I hold with my brother a Chief Scouts and Duke of Edinburgh award; Ronald flew planes just up until recently and I fly; Jasmine is English and my mum is English; my birthday is the 28th of August, Ronald's is the 28 of September; and lastly Ronald has a daughter called Anne Marie, my sister's name is Alison Marie. Over twenty plus years, we have remained close friends, helped and confided in each other. Ronald and Jasmine in recent years were able to go to an R.A.F auction in England and bring back a retired air force trainer, re-assemble the plane to New Zealand Civil Aviation requirements in existing R.A.F colors (Royal Airforce). Ronald and Jasmine are pilots and they would fly this De Havilland Chipmunk to air shows and vintage weekends around New Zealand for many years until hanging up their wings in 2019 and selling this and other vintage aircraft they had.

I had flown some commercial flights in their Piper Cherokee on many occasions and before leaving New Zealand would be flying for a company that did a considerable amount of aerial photography up and down both islands of New Zealand, the door being off the plane of course.

I also had some wild weekends with work colleagues in that time, who asked me to take them on a fishing trip to Great Barrier Island. Watch this space.

In Tauranga, I was able to work again for Tyco as they had an electrical branch in the area. I was initially asked to work on shift at a saw mill about an hour's drive from Tauranga in a place called

Tokoroa. I had a company car and was on salary plus overtime. There were three shifts, 7 am to 4 pm, 4 pm to 11 pm, 11 pm to 8 am. I had a week of each.

We had some fun times here. A fella who became a close friend of mine had just recently come to New Zealand with his family to escape the very declining economy of Zimbabwe. Trent became my offside also on our crew with a Canadian fella Derek. There was us and two fitters, Darell and Bruce. When you work with fitters, especially these fellas, anything out of the ordinary can happen.

The Saw Mill

Lord, shine your light on the path you have for me to travel. Help me to trust you are always with me.

There were a number of nights traveling to work on a night shift when we would be passing through some wild weather or coming home after a shift and I would come across an accident.

One night a massive big log had fallen across the road. Rounding the corner, we nearly drove straight into it. That night, we had to take some back roads to get to work.

Coming home after midnight, I was on a back country road. I came around a corner and a car was lengthways across the road, nearly T-boning it. I stopped. These fellas were trying to push the car off the road. They were both drunk. One fella had a gash across his head and was bleeding badly. I helped get the car off the road and waved down traffic in the dark with a torch.

I got the fella in the company car and offered to take him to a hospital. He was so drunk, all he wanted was to go home and that's where I went. There was blood all over the passenger's side. I realised why he didn't want to go to a hospital as police would have been called in and drunk driving charges would have been issued.

Next morning, I phoned the police and company to let them know what had happened.

On night shift one night, Trent and I had a repair to make in the operator's cab. This part of the operation rolled these relatively large logs on a carriage which the operator could move at some speed and turn the log between the carriage dogs or the sides of the carriage. The log itself would be moved through the big bandsaw which was the first part of cutting down logs into cut lengths of timber and from there it would be processed even further with special machines to graded cuts. Well, the operator's cab was like a play station except it was real. Trent and I fixed a broken switch on the operator's joy stick and decided we needed to see the carriage work as it had a log in it. We lost the log in the carriage, trying to spin it round. About 3 am, after three hours trying to get this log back on the carriage, we had to call in the big guns, "The Fitters." Did they have a laugh. They got a block and tackle, which has a chain and hook, to wrap around the log and a block which has a hook on it connected to a steel truss. Continuing to pull the chain on the block causes the hook to move up and lift the wait of the log. They then got the log back on the carriage within minutes. We never lived that one down.

We maintained breakdowns on the saw mill night and day on different shifts. Some of the bigger clients were from the USA, with some of the programs converted to feet and inches, as that is what the Americans work in.

There was a weekend planned when we were coming off a night shift. One of the fellas had a batch or holiday home on Great Barrier Island and I was asked if I could fly six of the fellas over to the island on a fishing trip for the weekend. It wouldn't be a problem. The island sits off Auckland in the Hauraki Gulf, an hour's flight from Tauranga. You fly up the coast and across the water to the island.

That Friday night, I loaded the first of the fellas with some fishing gear, fueled up, made a flight plan, sent it through to flight notifications, taxied out, and flew out to the island. Stage one for the afternoon completed. I arrived back at Tauranga Airport to pick the next few fellas up. First, I refueled and then asked these last three fellas how much gear they had. Their response was not much. Never believe a keen fisherman when he says that. These fellas were loaded with fishing gear. My weight and balance was on the verge of the plane being overweight with the center of gravity being on the limit. These fellas were in the back of the Cherokee, stacked with fishing gear on their laps and loaded to the ceiling.

We then started, received a taxi clearance and take off clearance. Utilizing most of the runway, I applied full power and started rolling down the runway. Using most of the length raised the nose and I climbed out just above the stall speed. The stall alarm came on intermittently as I climbed out slowly. This would be a pay load I would never attempt again for any flight.

Making a left hand turn towards the coastline, I assessed the time being in the air and the flight time to Great Barrier and realised we wouldn't make civil twilight. We were running late by about half an hour. There was no lighting at the Great Barrier airport so I made the decision to turn around, land, and fly out early in the morning. This would be Saturday morning early.

The fellas that were dropped off at Great Barrier first were able to utilise a local's vehicle to get to the holiday house and wait for us the next morning.

Saturday morning, I topped up with a gas but, without realizing it, I left the right hand fuel cap sitting on the wing. As we flew out the Saturday morning with a little less gear enough to make the fishing weekend enjoyable, we were flying up the east coast. I happened to be making flight checks and mental notes and noticed the fuel cap missing off the right hand tank. I didn't panic, just checked the right hand tank fuel gauge and made sure no fuel was being sucked out. All was OK. When we landed at Great Barrier, I immediately purchased a roll of duct tape. This covered and prevented any contamination for the ten hours flying to and from that weekend. The fuel cap was eventually found on the runway and returned. A new cap would have cost me and I learnt not to rush fuel then loading in and flying in restricted times for passengers.

We arrived at the island and were taken to the house. The fellas from there fished all day and all night. I watched a few movies, relaxed, went for a walk, and then went to bed.

With all the fish caught through the night and morning, the priority was to get the fish back on ice in a big eski (cooler) first. So the Sunday morning, I flew the fish back on ice, had it taken to a chiller plant, then flew back to get the first of two loads of passengers.

In Ronald's Cherokee 140, I flew ten hours for six keen fisherman with their rods and tackle that weekend. It would be the talking point at work for the next couple of days before I was asked if I would be interested in flying for the mile high club. Not knowing what this was at first, they just laughed at me. When I did find out, I was a bit taken back but had a laugh. These fellas were serious but with my standards, I acknowledged I would only do it if they were married.

The sawmill was a great place to work but within eighteen months, staff numbers were reduced and the company sent me to a pulp and paper plant with a new crew of fellas. This time, a company van would drive us to work.

Be happy with what you have while working for what you want.
— HELEN KELLER —

Working in heavy industry gave me an insight to machinery that were run by programs through variable speed drives, where you alter the current settings and frequency to allow machines, especially conveyors, to run fast or slow. These were run through PLCs or Program Logic Computer Systems, which go back to a control room monitor and every machine, pump, motor can be run or stopped from them. As a backup, you can utilise a remote station in the field where you drive machinery manually through a stop-start station. Also with pressure and flow instruments, you can measure exactly the amount of pressure or water flow per second powered up by 24v supply. The PLC modules for the transmitters would be in large cabinets in substations and where the main's power to verifiable speed drives that run the plant equipment are positioned. Programs can be updated by engineers or technicians, depending what the client's requirements are.

There were times these companies used my aircraft to fly for their projects or film expansions on sawmills and paper plants. And there were also times I flew to work using the company airstrip, landing, shutting down the aircraft, jumping fence and going to work. Sometimes I used to race the company van as it was a twenty-minute flight instead of one and a bit hours in the van. You actually flew over the mill and landed.

In an emergency, when equipment broke down or a part blew out, I would be asked to fly South to Napier where replacement parts would be ordered ahead. This day, I had flown in a light twin Piper Aztec to fly to Napier to pick up a part for a brand new VSD (veritable speed drive) that had been commissioned and had blown out. The drive itself was worth $60,000. The airstrip was used a lot when I was there but was decommissioned later as right at the very end of the airstrip, a steam gas turbine was installed to generate power for the company plant to reduce the amount of power charges paid to the government.

This is an area of steam and volcanic activity from the ground so there is plenty of steam to generate power from the ground surface.

This pulp and paper mill, or sawmill, is right next to a dormant volcano. The township is called Kawerau, the mountain is Mt Edgecumbe. When flying to and from work on a very fine day, you can see for hundreds of kilometers, seeing three very large dormant volcanos lined up. Mt Edgecumbe, Mt Tarawera, Mt Ruapehu, and vaguely in the distance Mt Taranaki way over on the west coast of the North Island.

Mt Tarawera exploded big time in the late 1800s, wiping out the pink and white terraces, and the lava decimated a Maori village, killing everyone, 120 people in all.

Mt Ruapehu exploded in 1995. I was in the air at the time and saw the whole mountain explode from the air. It was pretty impressive. Scheduled air traffic had to be diverted around the mountain for weeks, depending on which way the wind was blowing due to volcanic ash that could destroy turbine and piston engine aircraft. Ash travelled hundreds of kilometers for many months. If you left windows open in your house, everything inside would be covered with this grey ash dust, depending once again which way the wind was blowing. Our car and kitchen was covered with a fine coating of ash.

From the sawmill flying out to the coast is White Island. White Island is roughly twenty nautical miles off the east coast of the North Island and the closest township is Whakatane.

White Island is an active volcano and is monitored by volcanologists daily.

As you will be aware of the December 2019 tragedy, twenty-three people lost their life on the island due to the unpredictable activity of the volcano as it erupted. Many of my friends have made several trips to the island and now, due to the volcano tragedy, the island has been declared as a danger or no go zone.

All I can remember now is taking flight charters out to White Island and seeing the magnificence of the island from overhead and not in the direct path of any volcanic activity.

New Zealand has diverse and natural beauty and you have to travel around New Zealand to see this.

I am so thankful for my parents who showed us as a family travelling to many places in both North Island and South Island as well as Stewart Island growing up. And as they say, "DON'T LEAVE TOWN TILL YOU'VE SEEN THE COUNTRY."

The winter months are usually the wet and cold months of the year in New Zealand. It was during one of these weeks in May 2006 that a heavy weather depression had formed over the east coast and the amount of rain was very unusual. There had been massive slips and a runaway river with a massive amount of water had taken these huge and I mean huge boulders that were hundreds of years old and decimated part of a township and railway lines. We in the company van had been diverted around the lakes of Rotorua, resulting in a longer way home. The flood waters were over a meter deep on the coastal roads. A massive amount of civil and housing damage had resulted and a state of emergency had occurred at the time.

There were times I could possibly fly to work when the roads were blocked due to weather and if visibility was within 5000 meters and cloud base was 1000 feet or better, I was able to take off and land comfortably.

There were times of the year that I had to spend renewing my instrument ratings, flying solely on instruments on cross country exercise, joining designated holding patterns, making an approach with a simulated engine failure, making a missed approach and climbing out on one engine, requesting an on route clearance and flying back to destination having brought power onto the simulated dead engine. This had to be done every 180 hours or thirteen months, whichever came first. So in-between working and flying for company maintenance, I was working for Burns Aviation, flying low level photography up and down the North Island. We would load cameras and film kiwi fruit farmers and boundaries for clients, dairy farms, cattle stations, coastal ports, luxury resorts, wharfs, and city Center's right down both islands. Sometimes it meant flying under power lines at low level, through controlled airspace on request and clearances given. This would all be flown with the door off the plane between 300 and 1500 feet ASL (above sea level) as that is what the altimeter is set to on a barometric scale.

Despite the number of years I have flown, I have had only two emergencies, one losing VHF radio when the alternator failed. This meant radio communications with control center's was by phone and vectored into the airport. With the alternator out, all electrics was lost and I had to hand pump the undercarriage down and acknowledge lighting signals from the tower when approaching and landing.

The other incident was on an air transport flight out of Palmerston North, flying as co-pilot in the middle of an air traffic controllers' strike. With skeleton staff on most air traffic units including the military units, we were climbing into the clouds with eleven people on board and an air-force jet Macchi from nowhere cut right across our flight path within meters, no radio contact to advise where he was coming from.

An incident was filed but being military, they are not governed by civil aviation rules and the RNZAF only looked at the complaint.

The pulp and paper industry went through some major overhauls in the late 1990s and early 2000s. The paper production machines were massively overhauled with new technology to replace the 1960s technology. We worked night shift as the upgrade was 24/7, costing twenty-three million dollars. The sawmill at Kawerau was expanded by a Canadian company to diversify the logging mill cuts operation. As it was finished, the engineer and I flew a three-circuit run low level and high level, then came in on a ninety-degree angle from the east side with the door off the plane. The machinery was filmed from above and below in the mill operation and was placed on DVD for company records and also for promoting the company overseas. One of the best things thinking back to working at a saw mill was the smell of fresh pine tree cuts, the smell of timber. You have to have worked at a saw mill to understand what I mean. It was a great place to work and I think also that was one of the last times I flew in to the mill airstrip before it was decommissioned. An Israeli steam turbine was placed over a steam vent in the ground as I referred back to the volcanic activity and the power generated a power cost reduction.

My maintenance contract was up and from there was FIFO (fly in, fly out) for major projects in the South Island of New Zealand.

A new coal transfer station was being upgraded at Lyttelton Harbor, Christchurch.

Tyco had asked me if I would be interested in doing the upgrade, rewiring stackers and reclaimers and also the new coal conveyor tunnels at the port.

The coal trains came in from the west coast of the South Island, dumping coal on the car dumpers that transferred the coal on conveyors in the tunnels to coal stock yards, where the coal was graded on the stacker. Then on to the reclaimer and then on conveyors to the ship loader.

The reclaimer moves up and down the stock pile on railway tracks. Thus, with a cylindrical bucket of scopes turning all the time, it is able to load onto the conveyor to the ship. Our project was to wire in a PLC system in the new reclaimer for the programmers as well as the hard wire cabling systems on the reclaimer itself. We were then wiring in the remote sprinkler systems in the stock yards for water suppression sprinklers, then into the underground coal tunnels, running and wiring cables into steel conduits and terminating cables into explosive fittings, as coal and methane gases are highly explosive. As you can appreciate, we were covered in coal every night. Our clothes were lined with coal dust. I realise now for fellas who have worked in the coal environment for a number of years, BLACK LUNG IS A PROBLEM. This project was short term and even now, if I am working in the coal or any dusty environment, we wear respirators.

Tyco accommodated us in refurbished apartments in downtown Christchurch, in the exact buildings across the road from the bus station, the CBD that was tremendously damaged in the 2011 earthquake.

The building was very expensive inside. We shared a four-bedroom apartment with our own swipe cards for entry and to our own separate rooms. A movie theatre was provided with outside living spaces on all levels, and a massive big kitchen that a chief would be well pleased of.

On the weekends, I was able to go flying all over the Christchurch area with some of the engineers. One of the engineers happened to be an aircraft instrumentation and factory processing instrument technician, who had worked under contract for Lockheed aircraft in the USA.

I cannot remember his name, but a security pass to get into, not just one part of, Lockheed Aircraft but every part of the establishment was very hard to get. Your background checks were scrutinised for a week before you were eligible to work on one part of the plant only. Eventually, he saw them building the prototype of the stealth bomber, the flying wing which was a copy of the German designed Horton 29 jet from the Second World War. This aircraft was a jet and could not be picked up by radar. That was seventy-five years ago. Technology and some of that technology is still used today. Other aircraft being built were F18 fighter jets and he had a part in the instrumentation.

Traveling weeks at a time and living out of a suitcase, he sold up after twenty years and came back to New Zealand and worked a lower-paying job with Fletcher Challenge on the engineering side. This gave him time with his family and friends.

We worked at this project at Lyttelton for many weeks. We finished the cabling and power systems in the tunnels, we finished the cabling and wiring out the logics for the PLC systems on the reclaimer and the car dumper, which rotated each train carriage of coal till the unloading of all carriages was complete. We also finished off all the water dust suppression systems. We worked long and hard twelve hour days six days a week. It is what we do on all these industrial sites, including mines and gas and oil. The time spent away from home was five weeks for the first break. When we went on break, we were always flown to and from site with these projects. Being flown out of Christchurch, it was a good two-hour flight back to Tauranga.

My family was glad to see me home. I had two growing daughters who were at a young age and needed their dad.

When you are working on different projects or maintenance schedules for companies, you meet up with number of people and a number of contacts. It becomes a grapevine of work as a few of us look out for each other both on-site and off-site. Your phone numbers logged into your phone certainly builds up with company and colleague phone numbers and email addresses. This keeps our little communities of tradespeople in constant contact with each other for different work fronts. Many of these heavy industrial projects attract a variety of qualified persons from overseas and sometimes it seems you are working with the United Nations but as they say, variety is the spice of life, and many of these people are great to work with.

From the result of the expansion of the Lyttelton project, thousands more tonnes of coal were able to be shipped out as ships were continuously coming and going. I might add this is high grade coking coal, the same as they produce from the ground in Australia. It is used for making steel, not thermal coal which the Greenies don't understand and they drive around in their cars, build steel frames for housing and construction, and the list goes on. Steel is produced by a combination of cooking coal and iron with lime.

> *A man's heart plans his way but the Lord directs his steps.*
> *— PROVERBS 16.9 —*

I was back in Tauranga in the Bay of Plenty for the next six months, flying a number of hours, filming for Burns Aviation. One of Burns' cameramen was a Scotsmen. His name was Thom and I used to call him the flying Scotsmen. Thom had a broad Scottish accent and a good sense of humour. Thom or Burns would ring me the night before where and when they would be going to film. I would make arrangements to fly either out of Tauranga or over to a place called Matamata in the Waikato farming area. Now to fly to Matamata, you flew across the Kiami range. By the way, these are all Maori names, which defines New Zealand. Flying across the Kiami at low level was fun, directly out of the flight path of scheduled traffic and under secondary radar. You could stay close to tree top level. Immediately across the range, the terrain changed and it was flat green farming land. I would make a radio call as this aerodrome is uncontrolled and relies on a pilot's discretion, the direction he or she calls up from and intentions, as there could be a number of other aircraft in the vicinity. Parachuting and gliding is a big thing here at this aerodrome. The Matamata aerodrome is also a training place for academies over the summer months. So this area can get very active during the year.

We do have what they call NOTAMS notices to all airmen and areas designated on maps that are sent out when areas become active. You cannot fly through the active military areas unless you get special permission, which most often would never be granted unless it's an emergency. Burns had got himself into trouble one day flying near a sensitive military area. The plane was picked up on military radar and as soon as he landed, two military personal asked a few questions and removed his film from his aviation cameras.

Burns was a bit of a daring old fella. For his age, he was pretty active as he was seventy-nine years when I knew him.

Getting back to Thom, I picked him up in the plane from Matamata this day. As usual, the door was taken off and it was a cold winter's morning. I had my flying jacket on, and I was wearing wool boots to keep warm. Thom had selected his clients for the area and there were a few high-voltage power lines in the vicinity. As a pilot, you have to fly within the civil aviation regulations. There are minimum altitudes you can fly down to and you are responsible for every decision you make with the public, in this case passengers, in this case, the flying Scotsman.

These high voltage pylons are very tall and the power lines span hundreds of meters. 220,000 volts does give a big jolt. If you hit the lines, you could kiss your ass goodbye. Thom was filming in between three of these power lines at 300 feet. Remember the power line span has a big drop in the middle and would be close to 400 feet to the bottom of the span from the ground ASL. I flew low, within 150 feet off the base of that span three times to get his camera positions right, keeping a constant lookout for any other obstructions below. Eventually, I cleared the power lines and climbed back up to 2000 feet. From there, I proceeded around the base of the Kiami range then flew north to the Hauraki Gulf and back to Matamata. Between two and two-and-a-half hours in the air would be enough time before Burns or Thom would start running low on film.

The flying Scotsman, having worked for a number of years for Burns, got very sick and passed away within the three years I had known him. That was a sad day. An end of an era.

Prior to all this, I had been studying towards a C-cat instructor's rating. This had taken a lot of my spare time as you had to know and explain the physics of flight, teach a lesson with a briefing on the board and then fly and teach in the air. This is also a good way to overcome your fears when standing up and speaking in front of a number of people. This whole exercise required a number of hours in a classroom, thirty hours in the air flying and teaching and a government flight test with a testing officer.

I also had to spend time with family and even now thinking about it, having lived in Tauranga for those few years, there were fun places I had never been to and it's only in recent times that I have been to these places when visiting, such as Mac Lauren's Falls, and Kiami Range Falls just to name a few.

Life has a way of catching up. Sometimes you become too busy. You don't have time to wake up and smell the roses.

There were times I just had to say no in the end, just had to have that break and time out and go away for a holiday.

The end of the year had come and I had damaged my leg in an accident at work. Vijaya and I had saved a little money and decided to take our girls Rachel and Cilla to Fiji for Christmas and just rest up a bit. Vijaya still had family there, a brother and sister. It would be good, we thought, for our girls to meet their cousins of a similar age they hadn't met and of course Vijaya had been with me a couple of years ago and had sat quietly in an interview with Air Pacific, now Fiji Airways.

I was a little crippled at the time we rocked up at Auckland Airport for a flight with Korean Airlines. I played on my sore leg with the staff as they felt sorry for me and, yes, because of my condition (it wasn't as bad as I had made it out to be) they seated us all as a family in business class, which I had been hoping for. Making sure I had my leg in a position the hostess could see I needed constant looking after, with Vijaya in the seat next to me. Vijaya thought the attention-seeking was a little funny but it did work.

Well, you should have seen the smile on the girls' faces: big seats, lots of room, the hostess bringing them refreshments in the air, a little TV screen for themselves and Father Christmas happened to be sitting in the seat across the ways from them. I've never seen a Korean Santa before.

We arrived in Fiji, greeted by family and friends. Man, it was hot, "BULLA VANAKA" in Fijian. We immediately proceeded to the township of Lautoka from Nadi. The area is made up of a lot of sugar cane farms, a lot of happy smiling Fijians and a lot of hard working curry munchers, I mean Fijian Indians. Pretty relaxed. I think it was about three days before Christmas and we were hitting the markets, Vijaya was negotiating prices in Hindi as she does, finding the right bargains. The girls and I were having a bit of fun in the local shops. We wanted to dress Vijaya up in a Indian Sari, very colorful. I tell you, this is Bollywood in Fiji and she does look great in a Sari.

If you like curries, there is no shortage of this in our Indian community. You get to be invited to all the relatives in the villages and in the township on the island..You can just live off of curries for breakfast, lunch and dinner. And the best thing about them is this food is very healthy.

We went out to the other islands, snorkeling and diving in the sun and, as they say, FIJI: THE WAY THE WORLD SHOULD BE. It was a great day. Lunch was included in the boat fare to and from the island.

On Christmas Day, my brother-in-law swallowed a small meat bone and it got lodged in his throat. He was choking. We managed to give him the Heineken method. I was behind and used my arms at the front to pull up under his ribs to cause the bone to dislodge. It did but was still stuck in his throat. This was causing him to breathe heavy. We drove him to the hospital and went to emergency. The fella was still gasping for air. The old doctor came down, had a look, and says to us, "He will have to come back for an operation on Friday." WHAT: This is Wednesday afternoon and the fella is still breathing heavy. Someone else came racing into the hospital within minutes after us and this fella had a heart attack and died. So we raced out of the hospital down to the port. I knew the YWAM (youth with a mission) Mercy Ship was in at the port and had a nurse on board. I had worked and refitted electrically the galley on this boat in recent months in New Zealand. We called, told her we were coming, and she met us coming onto the boat. The nurse quickly got him to the clinic and got some dried rice which she gave him to try and swallow. It slowly dislodged the bone. He was eventually able to cough the bone up.

You never know what's going to come up next. We spent a good two weeks on the main island, Veta Levu. We went to the movies, swam a lot, cooked a lavu in the ground, traditional Fijian style. This is cooking in the ground with hot stones, covered with banana leaves. The Maori in New Zealand call it a Hangi, very similar.

Talking about Hangi's in Gisborne, a few years earlier I was working in a Housing New Zealand complex and this complex had the Mongrel Mob living in it. This is a Maori gang. I must admit they were very clean. They asked me, "Bro, can you wire out our shed and put security lights on our gates?" No problem, you pay me cash? "OK, bro." Then they said to me, "Hey, bro, we are having a fundraiser, Hangi, you want to buy a ticket, bro? $5." I said, "OK," and ended up helping them getting the food. Then they said, "Bro, come back at 5 pm." I came back at 5 pm. "Bro, we've rung out of Hangi. Come back tomorrow night." This was so funny, I didn't really mind either way.

I flew back early to New Zealand for work. Vijaya and the girls stayed for another week. When I flew in and out of New Zealand after the first two years of Dad being home from his incarceration in Peru, my bags were never on the baggage conveyor. I had to find them at the baggage claim office. The locks were off and I knew my bags had been searched. I had this terrible feeling that Dad and I were still being investigated for any drug dealing by the New Zealand police and customs. I can still remember Mum and Dad's phone being tapped by the New Zealand police for a number of months after Dad had come home. You could hear the click click. Dad had never any criminal records or convictions against him and should have been acknowledged by Interpol and the New Zealand police for his services abroad. Having to come back and explain himself was one thing and at the same time he had lost everything. People would rather gossip and spread rumours than know the truth.

A week later, I drove up to Auckland, New Zealand and picked my family up, having arrived back from Fiji.

The Lord is restoring all your wasted years
He's giving you a reason to smile again.
You will see better days. Amen.

In the years to come, my family would again face some challenges, many of them good, before leaving New Zealand in July 2006.

I began working a few maintenance shutdowns, electrical work at the pulp and paper plants, Kawerau and Kinleith, and in between times flying for Burns Aviation, flight charters. When I say maintenance shutdowns, I mean part of the plant is taken out of commission to do work on it. Once maintenance is completed, all locks are taken off the electrical and mechanical isolation points.

Everything is electrically and mechanically tested and equipment is placed back into service. I continued with maintenance work for the next five months until a company called Downer Engineering signed me on a milk dryer construction contract in the Deep South of New Zealand, South Island. The number three milk dryer at CLANDEBOY was being built for a New Zealand dairy company FONTARA. This was just twelve kilometers from the Township of Timuka.

We were flown from Tauranga to Christchurch, New Zealand and driven to the Township of Timuka. Each day, we were bused to site. We were accommodated in an old hotel in Timuka and all our allowances were going to pay for the accommodation and food at that hotel. This was in the middle of winter and it was cold and snowing. One smart fella had the idea of going to the camping ground and lodging in a caravan. He saved more than half of his living away allowance for each week he was paid, so we thought we would go and try the caravan thing as well. Never been so cold in all of my life. Had a mattress on the floor of the caravan, a small heater, slept with my clothes on, two blankets over me, and was still cold. In the morning, a tap outside had been dripping and bits of ice had formed on the droplets. That's how cold it was. The days were fine and cold but every few days, it would snow.

Now on this crew, we had some interesting characters. We had Pot Head Pete. Pete had an unfortunate case of depression and his only remedy, as I recall, was his medical marijuana, which of course wasn't. His whole room at the motel was a mess with it and he got kicked out in the end, having to pay someone to clean up his mess. We had to cover for him on site all the time and fix up his electrical work, yet we still liked him and did the best we could for him. Today no one is allowed on any major site with drugs in their system. The screening is tested for drug and alcohol before you go on site. You either pass or fail. We had Malcolm who used to wind everyone up to get a reaction but was a good electrician.

There was an Aussie bloke who used to come flying with me down the South Island. I cannot remember his name. Then there was Barry who would sneak around the whole site before security came in. He pinched all the scrap copper on site, then took it down to the scrap metal man in a company van and sell after hours.

We had a couple of TA's (trade assistance). One was a driving instructor and I will tell you a little story shortly with him. The other TA kept much to himself. The rest of the fellas were contractors to Downer Engineering under the management of John L.

The milk dryer itself was about forty levels. You didn't want to forget any electrical equipment if you were working right at the top. We were powering up all heavy machinery and mcc and substations as well as the local control boxes in the field.

One morning going to work, I was driving the company van. I had the driving instructor TA with me and was approaching this corner which was called CHICKEN AND HAM CORNER. I didn't know why it was called that but I soon found out why. My driving instructor TA said to me, "You better slow down," questioning why as I was only travelling at 60 km and slowing to 50 km/h. I hit that corner and did a 180-degree spin into oncoming traffic on black ice. That's why it was called CHICKEN AND HAM CORNER. Fortunately, no accident prevailed as the line of traffic stopped before any damage could be done.

That was my second experience spinning on black ice. The first one was on the Canadian freeway.

On the weekends, I was able to access a Cherokee-180 light aircraft, taking engineers from on site to observe the project from the air. There were weekends I would be flying company charters up and around Mt Cook, around the glacier lakes and alongside the Franz Joseph glacier. The terrain was high and temperatures very cold, but the sites were spectacular for the cameraman. We were flying for a short time up to 14,000 feet unpressurised to the face of Mt Cook, the air being very thin. You can appreciate we had to be careful of our oxygen requirements. This mountain is one of the highest peaks in the South Island, white capped with snow all year round. Then we flew down to the base of the mountain and across the glacier Lake Tekapo. It was two hours flying around mountainous terrain then flying back to Timaru Airport where temperatures were a little warmer and the small amounts of ice that had accumulated on the windscreen and fuselage started to melt away. Also we were flying back down to sea level.

The fellas talked about this adventure all week and couldn't wait to have flight plans lodged to fly down to Queenstown and fly around the Remarkables, which were the mountains surrounding Queenstown and Lake Whakatipu.

Unfortunately, the weekend we had planned to fly, we were all called back into work to start commissioning the Milk Dryer. WATCH THIS SPACE. THERE IS ANOTHER TRIP COMING. AND A BIG ONE.

There were other weekends we did manage to take the company van tripping around the Deep South. We went to places like Twizel, which is a township that had been built as temporary accommodation in the late 1960s for workers on the construction of dams and power stations on the Waitaki river. Twizel has remained as a township and hosts many tourist attractions, including trout fishing in the canals that lead to the lake and great scenery. We drove through and had fish. We saw the trout but it was always the fish that got away. We drove to Lake Tekapo. I had mentioned this previously, having flown over. Here inland from Tekapo was a ski field and a few of us hired some skis. We caught the chair lift up and went skiing down the mountain. We spent a half a day here on the slope in the sun and fresh snow and then did a big loop towards the coast. Again we hit black ice along the road in the shaded areas but did not succumb to it, although we did get out of the van and walked across the road, doing a few spins.

The back country of the South Island is a collector's dream. There are old Army trucks parked up, old vintage cars ready to be restored. Farmers never throw anything away down here. I knew of a fella in Nelson, a farmer who bought a decommissioned Dehavilland mosquito aircraft off the RNZAF many years ago. He keeps it in a shed and fires it up every so often. There was no buyer who could offer enough money for this aircraft and also a P51 mustang that he had as well. To the farmer, it was priceless. This man would be very aged now or may be passed on.

This generation of eccentrics are a dying breed and with our generation, it is up to us to remember the past and past mistakes, not to dwell on the past but learn from the past and remember history.

Back on site, the first four weeks were going good until I had a slight accident. I was working on level forty of the milk dryer and had a TA working with me. I don't think he was too bright. He asked for certain electrical items we needed, then he just disappeared. I had to go and get the switching gear myself and in my rush to get to the container and back up top, I tripped over a concrete slab. I knew I had done some damage. I had damaged my ligaments in my leg. My leg just went black from the knee down with swelling on top of that. I had to go to the hospital to get it looked at and dressed. Being close to my break, the company flew me home to Tauranga for ten days off.

The swelling remained and when I returned to work after those ten days, I was sent to a doctor who sliced my leg open and relieved the pressure by draining the blood. After that and having it dressed every day, it came good.

These next few weeks were the finishing off on the Downers part of the contract. We were working in the redlined areas where we had to suite up with white sperm suits. gloves, masks and boot covers. Even our tools had to be sprayed to prevent any bacteria coming into this processed part of the milk dryer. A small job of terminating or testing would take about two hours instead of twenty minutes.

And of course we had to take everything off, I mean, protection gear we were wearing when we came out. Commissioning of the mcc and substations were the most time consuming as we were point to point testing. We had one person out in the field and one person in the switch room with a meter and the person in the field would bridge a circuit out with a bit wire and my meter would pick up that deflection to identify the circuit. We would be using two-way radios or mobile phones to communicate.

It was on this day we were doing this testing that a fella flew over us in a light aircraft and crashed directly into the sea.

We finally left the milk dryer project in November 2004 and saved a bit of a cash from working weeks away. Before we left, every Thursday night in Timuka, a karaoke bar was open and it was a company requirement that we had to prove we could sing. We could sing anything we wanted. Well, there are a few guys who could sing and others whose vocals had a rough passage out. Pothead Pete simply topped it. He could sing some of Jimmy Hendrix's songs well. I was not too far behind with Rod Stewart's I AM SAILING. The other fellas, well, they had fun getting the lyrics out. It was a good time. I can say life is what you make it. Create an attitude of happiness and great fullness even in rough times or you can be miserable and someone else is always the problem. I choose the first.

Every place, project, emergency run I have been involved with have tried to make another person's life better.

Next day, I flew home.

> *Success is not final, failure is not fatal.*
> *It is the courage to continue that counts.*
> — WINSTON CHURCHILL —

We all fail in life at something or other. It's when we have the courage to get up and go again and again and again, keeping our goals in sight and not losing that passion, that we attain success. It might not be instant. It might take a few years but if we remain focused, we will achieve great things that make the world a better place.

My interaction with people of all walks of life over the years gave me the confidence to speak in front of groups, and listen to people's ideas. Also by studying how successful people overcame their failures, I have been able walk through problems I have faced with their mentorship.

The reason I am taking time to talk about courage and determination is that the younger generation needs to know and learn from problems that we face in life and not be shielded from them. Just as important, our generation needs to learn from millenniums.

Life sucks sometimes. My father was set up as a drug smuggler. Two of my friends were killed in aviation accidents. So called friends I had known for a long time had used all my resources and left me broke. My sister suffered from anorexia nervosa and nearly died. My best friend, a Canadian, died of cancer. Did I feel bitter? No. Did I feel sad? Yes. Did I harbour resentment? A little, at first. Did I forgive? Yes. I don't wish people to go through those experiences but I am sure everyone will face some challenges in life.

With some of these challenges, I had to be honest with myself as well and true to my convictions. If I compromise, I reduce my standards. Having integrity, a faith in Christ, and seeing the best in others—it will actually surprise you as these values exist in a world of shifting values. There are people who will become good friends because they know you care. They have their best interests at heart and yours theirs.

My family is special to me and when they know I have had to go away working a few weeks at a time, they know I am providing for them.

When they need security, I provide for their security. When there is a family crisis, we try and work together to solve it.

When a friend is in trouble, we are there to listen or help if required.

Again I like to word another one of Winston Churchill's quotes: *Attitude is a little thing that makes a big difference.*

In this part of the story, I will say I am thankful for every day, every experience, and every adventure. Never limit yourself to what you can achieve. When there is an obstacle, find a way around it. When you find you cannot go any further, stop and reevaluate the situation. When you need encouragement, seek those who will cheer you on.

In recent times, I have had to re-evaluate my situation.

Importantly, I take time to smell the roses. We all need to take time out. Our bodies need to rest. We are not designed to keep working and working. Our bodies will eventually break down or tell us to slow down. Or else it will shut down.

Lord, shine your light on the path you have for me to travel. Help me to trust you are always with me.

Arriving back in Tauranga November 2004, I was able to renew some of my multi-engine aircraft endorsements. This allowed me to fly private charters out to White Island (volcanic activity) and out to some of the other islands off the Bay of Plenty for a group of people.

The other trip we were planning for over the coming Christmas break was being a leader for a group of young people working towards their Duke of Edinburgh Gold achievement. This would involve paddling 180 km down one of the central rivers in the North Island of New Zealand, the Wanganui River. We had secured fourteen kayaks and one Canadian canoe. The Canadian canoe took all our supplies, food tents, and cooking equipment. And kayaks, of course, taking our basics. This would be our change of clothes in waterproof bags, light refreshments, and drinking water.

The trip was very well-planned as we would be bused down to the head of the river from a place called Taumarunui, a small township in the central North Island. The driver of the bus would pick the group up at a place 180 kms down the river called Piperiki, which is a small settlement on the east bank of the Wanganui river. The trip itself would take a week.

The Maori people along this river are known as the river people, they are the custodians of the river and many Maori songs have come from the generations of these people. It wouldn't be unusual to see a few traditional Maori war canoes paddling down this river, as we were told.

Everything was well-arranged in the weeks before Christmas. Neil Turner, Ian Batemen, James Turner, a Swiss chef Peter and I led the group of young people.

So there was a team of about fifteen. Five leaders and ten mature young people. There had been heavy rain over the last two weeks before we left for the journey and this made the river very swollen in parts. There were the naysayers who said we should not go because it was too dangerous with that amount of water and we would be forced or tipped out of our kayaks. This would not be true of course as we got to the starting point of the river on a very sunny day. The conditions were better than we expected and we launched all kayaks and canoes immediately.

We all teamed up and had a bit of a chat on staying together. We prepared everyone in three groups, life jackets on. One group of three would remain in front, four kayaks in the middle and the remainder tail end Charlie. This worked out well. Along the river at certain points were Department of Conservation (DOC) camping grounds we could use for camping. There were also some other international tourists who had decided to team up with us as well.

The first day down the river, we travelled about 27 km per day. The water was fast-moving although we hadn't got to the big rapids as yet. We camped at the first camping ground. We cooked all our own meals. We were pretty tired but feeling really good for the first night. Most of us had a good night's sleep. The Swiss couple that were with us that night were going for it in the tent next to us. In the morning, Ian Bateman happened to pass the comment, "Did you sleep OK last night? There were a lot of noises in the tent next door." Yep, I heard it too.

Day two, we had breakfast at 6.30 am, packed up camp, and placed all kayaks and canoes in the water. This day we had jet boats coming up the river in the opposite direction. These boats can move on inch of water. (The Hamilton jet engine was designed in New Zealand).

We had a few rapids to face. We all experienced enough to ride through the rapids with a couple of the young people rolling out and getting back into kayaks. This would be called a category two river. The river was getting a little stronger but it wouldn't be till the third and fourth day tthat we would be hitting the best that the Wanganui river could throw at us.

It was always a good time to stop for a lunch break, regroup, and talk about how the day was going. No one was sick or injured, we were all fighting fit to face any challenge.

Camping the second and third night at completely different DOC camping grounds, our Mr Chef started to help us put some extra flavours into our cooking. His kitchen peaks when he takes control of a kitchen on a Moari Marae on day six to cook for the whole community.

There were Maori Village Maraes along the way. A Marae is a Maori meeting house where they have celebrations, community meetings, meals outside, sleeping. The Maori people are very accommodating, as I will point out later in the trip.

Day four, I hit a rapid, a very hard rapid. It spun me right over and back upright, a complete 180 degree flip but I kept my hat on in this fast moving water. Up ahead, there had been a traditional Maori war canoe moving down the river, drifting out of sight.

Paddling into calmer waters, we stopped and waited for everyone in the team to catch up. As we pulled up, we watched this other Canadian canoe with two tourists in it hit these same rapids. They lost control, hitting the rapids side on. They flipped the canoe and were just managing to hold on till they came into calmer waters near us. We were able to help them turn their canoe back over. Fortunately for them, their belongings were securely strapped down in the canoe.

We made it through the fourth day, no casualties or broken bones, and camping this night on a hill above the river, averaging around 26 km per day. There's a lot of good scenery down this river and wild life, native bush. Fortunately there are no snakes or crocks down here in this part of the world as there are in Australia.

That night we were pretty relaxed. We had fun just talking and telling jokes, although we didn't have any marshmallows to toast around the fire.

Day five, we had an excursion trip to a tourist attraction called the Bridge to Nowhere. This is a big concrete bridge in the middle of the bush way up above a ravine. We parked our kayaks up on the embankment. We had to climb over some hills to come to a valley, then an old overgrown kind of road that I'm sure many years ago had been a lot wider. There wasn't much between the edge of the road and a sheer drop below into a big gorge or valley. At the top of the road track was the arched concrete bridge.

The story goes that this bridge was built for an old farmer in the 1930s during the Great Depression so he could get to and from his farm with bridging access. The bridge was built and after it was built, he decided to shift into town. Thus it was the bridge to nowhere. The bridge itself had been overgrown for many years until recent times. You can walk across it or run across it, whatever rocks your boat. The concrete structure has been very well-preserved over the years as the concrete arch below looked as though it had been built yesterday.

That was a good four hours. As we were coming and going, there were two jet boats with tourists coming up and flashing their cameras.

There was only one wet day down the river. The rest of the days were sunshine and blue sky. The day to the bridge to nowhere was the day I think it rained.

From our excursion, we jumped back into our kayaks, James Turner leading the way with three, Neil Turner and myself in the middle with four, Ian and the Cheff in the Canadian canoe with the remaining three alongside. By day five, we had paddled 100km or so. By this time also, our German friends had paddled on ahead and we said Auf Wiedersehen and we never saw them again.

On the sixth day, we hit some wild rapids. These would be the last of the many and the water was running fast. We hit them hard and we came out hard. We all made it through. No damage, just wet and adrenaline junkies, just a few cheers and WOOHOO.

I tell you what, that adrenaline junkie is still in me today. These young bucks really enjoyed themselves.

Getting close to Wanganui Heads is where the river meets the Tasman Sea and becomes tidal. That night we camped on the Marae grounds. Better facilities there than the DOC camping ground. That night, the locals came out and greeted us officially on their Marae. It was a large gathering. When you greet a male on a Marae, a hongi hongi is a touching of noses and for the woman, a kiss. I was touching noses with one fella, thinking this other person was a woman except he was a young man with long hair. I gave him a kiss. He stepped back, I stepped back, and I wasn't even a cross dresser. That was on another Marae on the east coast. So this time I had to be touching noses with the right person and kissing the right woman.

That was all good and Peter the Chef really excelled himself that night cooking for the community as well as ourselves. He was given all the food and his preparation was commendable. That was a good night. We didn't go to bed till late, no camp fire that night, we were just entertained by the locals. They put on a Maori concert party and these people can sing. Eventually we did go to bed but didn't leave till a bit later the next morning as we were a little tired. We had the last leg of our journey, the last 25 km.

We were all a bit blurry-eyed that morning and I think no one talked much on the last part of the paddle. We had been through all the rapids now and we were facing a little of the tidal challenge. Fortunately, Piperiki wasn't too far down the river and we could make it by mid-afternoon. The show was just about over and we would have completed 180 km and everyone intact.

We did reach Piperiki with the bus driver and a late lunch all prepared. That was great.

Having had lunch, we packed up all the equipment on the trailer and said our goodbyes to the locals before driving home.

LEAVING THE EAST COAST OF NEW ZEALAND

These young people were great. Having achieved a Duke of Edinburgh Gold award myself, I know what an achievement it is for young people. It shows commitment, determination, and never quitting. We arrived back in Tauranga late that night as it was a five-hour trip back.

We thanked God for his protection and safety.

> *A day without laughter is a day wasted.*
> —CHARLIE CHAPLIN —

With my friends Ronald and Jasmine in Tauranga and also my Zimbabwean friends Trent and Ange, we were all there for each other. Ronald had commercial properties he rented out with long term clients. There were buildings he was renovating and often would need power and light circuits either installed or re-circuiting. We would both work together to get the electrical done and Dad would have a little building project he could help with as well. Sometimes I would come off a night shift just to help for a few hours as needed before taking a nap.

One of the projects we did all together—Ronald, Dad, and I—was a refit to the heating system and modified toilet block for a historical Anglican Church. This was Ronald and Ange's place of worship. The surrounding area had been a battleground between the Maori tribes and the British 150 years prior, known as the battle of Gate Pa. The British of course had winched all their heavy guns up the hill from the ships and the Maori war party had imbedded themselves in trenches. As the British shelled and shelled the Maori positions, thinking they had decimated the Maori, the Maori war party had entrenched themselves under fire and came out and annihilated the British forces. There is a picture painted of a lone Maori woman holding and giving a dying British soldier something to drink. Underneath the picture, it says, "IF YOUR ENEMY THIRSTS, GIVE HIM SOMETHING TO DRINK," the words of Jesus in the gospel of Matthew. The stream is still there.

There is a lot of interesting history in New Zealand as the Maori have been there for over 1000 years.

Ronald, Jasmine, and I flew together, if they were not tripping around the country flying in for airshows or going overseas on conferences.

With Trent and Ange, we would be out in the bush somewhere on a weekend or lapping up the sun on the beaches in the summer with our families. There was always something we were doing together in our downtime. When we did have downtime. Barbecues, dinners, fun parks.

A group of us from the Salvation Army Church in Tauranga planned a white water rafting trip in the Tongariro National Park in the centre of the North Island of New Zealand. The Salvation Army had an outdoors facility for outdoor pursuits, including white water rafting and caving.

The next few months in between working and flying, we were fundraising to take as many fellas as we could down the Tongariro River and caving. We had garage sales and sausage sizzles. I think we may have even had gold coin donation fun night.

Anyway, we raised the money, $2000 for the whole weekend, the fuel for the bus, hiring the instructors and camp facilities in the middle of winter. So one weekend in June 2005, all ten of us left on a Friday afternoon, heading for Tongariro Camp, Salvation Army facilities. Arriving at the camp around 9.00 pm, I settled in for the night in the dorms allocated.

I have to say, one of the most tragic things going to sleep or trying to go to sleep is in a dorm with a person who snores heavily. The noise vibrates around all four walls. Even a pillow won't silence the noise. Our snoring person was our cook Dave so we had to give him a bit of a break.

We did get some sleep and that Saturday morning, we were up at a reasonable hour. We had breakfast, had morning devotions, then we were preparing the white water rafts and wet suits for the trailers. We left around 7.30 am to get to the head of the Tongariro

River. This is a category 3 river and when they flood, it can even go higher.

With the instructors being with us, I think for some of the fellas, it was their first time they had been on a white water rafting trip. So the briefing about holding on inside the raft, what happens if anyone falls out or the raft tips, was very important. We got into our wet suits, life jackets, and helmets in preparation for launching the three rafts into the water. Ian Bateman, Trent, Big Dave, and I were in one raft with an instructor. All the other fellas were split up into the other three rafts with an instructor in each raft and we started to move. We did move very quickly with the rushing current. If you want an adrenaline rush, white water rafting is something great to do. You can expect someone or two to fall as they did along the river, but the idea is not to panic as your life jacket will keep you afloat and wet suit will keep you insulated. The rapids were exceptional, maneuvering around them was great and flying straight over the falls and landing back on the water, watching to see if anyone is going to fall out and yes they did. We had some big guys including Big Dave who held on pretty good. We were paddling pretty hard as well. Some of the expressions on the fellas' faces were so funny.

It was a good one-and-a-half hours down the raging part of the river till we got into calmer flowing water. Everyone was enjoying the moment. Photos were being taken and we got to sing a few songs along the way. These fellas had better voices than fellas at the Karaoke bar down the South Island that night.

We kept paddling down the calmer part of river. The greenery was providing a sheltered canopy over the river itself. Even in the calmer parts, there was a substantial amount of water flowing, just not as fast.

The Tongariro River flows down through Turangi to Lake Taupo, a very big lake. We didn't go right down through to Turangi but we covered a central part of the Tongariro River. I can say that down the river, there are lots of trout as well and keen fisherman at Turangi Township end.

All in all, it was a great day. Most of the day was spent on the water. We had lunch set up for us at the pickup point, a number of kilometers down the river.

Taking our wet suits off, drying off, we were able to get into some dry warmer clothes and had lunch.

The camp staff reloaded the trailers with the rafts and the rest of the gear as we were enjoying lunch.

We drove in the two vans back to the camp, arriving back about late afternoon.

I have to admit, you can really break down barriers when you get a few guys together, some not knowing others at first but when we begin to share together and look out for each other you start some great friendships and that was the whole purpose of the weekend.

The weekend was not over yet. We had a caving expedition coming up next. The following day would be venturing into the bowels of the earth.

Big Dave had the kitchen that night and Dave's kitchen ruled. We helped prepare but he wouldn't let us anywhere near the cook up. Never trust a skinny cook. Dave was a bit larger than a skinny cook so his masterpieces should be OK, I thought. We weren't disappointed, spaghetti and meatballs and there was plenty of it. Dave excelled himself with producing a hot sweet pudding. THREE CHAIRS for Dave and he got it.

Then reality set in. We had to go to sleep in the same dorm again as Dave and I didn't know if it was the dinner or extra exertion of the day's activities but the snoring reached a massive crescendo and the walls took a hammering as well as Ian, Trent, and my eardrums.

We did get to sleep eventually and Dave's snoring toned down a bit.

The next morning, being a Sunday, we were up at a reasonable hour, 7.00 am, to have breakfast, devotions, and prepare for the caving expedition. By 8.30 am, we had to pack all the gear, overalls, helmets, lights and emergency lights, as you can well-appreciate.

We drove about half hour to the cave entry. We got and

assembled all our gear, and checked our batteries for our headlamp and emergency lights. We made sure our boots were tight and carried some water with us.

We then preceded through the small entrance with our two guides down into the cave lights all ablaze, following a stream going quite a ways down. By the way, if you ever want to find your way out of a cave, always follow water uphill. We were going down into the belly of the cave and coming another way out. It seemed a long way down by the time we got down to this cavity. We had to crawl through this very small crack, body width, to crawl through. We had to pull some of the bigger fellas through, including Big Dave. Some of the fellas were a little petrified being in small enclosed areas. We just reassured them that the ground wasn't going close in on them at this time.

We got into this big open cavity and the guide told us to switch our cap lamps off. Complete darkness. The guide asked how we felt. There was complete silence for a minute. I am not sure if everyone was in shock or lost for words. Then someone said, "It's a bit dark in here, isn't it?" and everyone laughed.

We then switched our lights back on and crawled out of the cavity. We walked even further down into the earth before we made a slight detour to come back up. Everyone was accounted for. We had lost no one to a crack in the wall. We were even proud of Big Dave and Ian. Ian was a big strong fella as well.

I remember years ago in the scouts, one of the scout leaders was in the New Zealand Speleologist Society and he led us caving underground. We started with waterfall drop in the middle of the bush going down on a steel ladder. I went down first and ran out of ladder so had to climb back up and get the ladder extended and then go down again, waiting for everyone to climb down.

We then were told we had to chimney our way back up through the crack in the wall all the way up. Well, you have never seen all these young bucks, including me, move so quick through that crack. It was as if they thought the earth was going to move and they would be stuck in the wall. We also did crawl through and down underground streams there as well.

We changed directions underground, walking back upstream, following another river that twisted and turned for quite a ways. I cannot remember feeling very cold under there, just wet and uncomfortable, but bearable. There were no complaints by any of the fellas, whether they were still in a state of shock or just happy to keep moving. Either way it was all good and we did eventually make it back up to the top in the early part of the afternoon.

We had spent around six hours underground by the time we reached the surface.

In years to come, I would spend many hours underground working as a High Voltage Electrician in the Australian mining industry, down to about 2000 meters in the ground but with working areas and workshops all lit up. Also working underground in a gold mine in Western Australia just recently, turning my cap lamp off and in the complete darkness, I revisited the same experience in the cave that day we turned our cap lamps off and sat in complete darkness. I will touch on that at the end of the book.

We made it to the top and imagine the smile on these guys' faces. Some of them had stepped outside their comfort zone and the rest of the fellas had done similar adventures on different continents around the world but the New Zealand experiences ranks one of the best.

I think Big Dave was in the mindset of preparing lunch and had a new lease of life. Ian also rose to the occasion.

We enjoyed a late lunch with the staff, compliments of Big Dave. I think this might have been a long weekend, so we didn't have to rush back to Tauranga that night.

We went back to the camp, cleaned up, had a shower. That night we had an informal debrief on how everyone was feeling. I asked everyone in turn their thoughts of the trip, if there was anything they didn't enjoy and what they would like to do next. There were no complaints just great camaraderie. We had a devotional time and a

LEAVING THE EAST COAST OF NEW ZEALAND

thank you prayer.

Dave once again excelled himself in the kitchen, no spaghetti or meatballs this time but a nice beef stew that fed us all nicely. I think he may have timed it right to cook a spongey pudding. Big Dave was a champ.

That night we were all tired and went to bed early. Dave managed to regroup himself and was able to sleep a little on his side to prevent that dreadful snoring. The other team members in the dorm next to us were quiet as well.

Monday morning, we made the trip home to Tauranga. We were up around 7.00 am. Showered and had breakfast. Then we packed all our gear and personal belongings back into the van.

By 8.30 am, we had said our goodbyes and farewells and were on the road. On the way home, we stopped just outside a village called Raurimu. Here you can find a viewing platform where you can view a train spiral, called the Raurimu spiral. This is an engineering masterpiece built in the late 1880s. You can watch a train spiraling up the mountain whilst going through the mountain at different levels till it gets to the top. Cuts out 8 km of track from bottom to top and this is on the main trunk line of the North Island, train going north to south. It's in the middle of the North Island. Pretty amazing to watch a train go through.

From there we had lunch and we were home about 4.30 pm.

Thoroughly recommend white water rafting on a bucket list. Another adventure done.

Be good to people. You will be remembered more for your kindness than any level of success you could possibly attain.
— MANDY HALE —

In the months to follow in 2005, the heavy industrial plants kept downsizing.

Government selling off assets into the private sector to generate a quick fix cash flow for their stimulus packages. The pulp and paper industry markets were changing and taxes on these companies were increasing. The problem was these big companies would downsize and take their production or resources to a more affordable market place overseas. Not just New Zealand but other industrialised countries as well. Where labour was cheap is where they went. This had an effect on a lot of trades and engineering staff, including myself. We were placed on short-term contracts with no benefits. To me this didn't matter much as, having been a contractor for many years, I knew how a system worked and also how to generate extra income outside my primary source of income. But to a lot of other trades, people, and qualified engineers, they didn't have this luxury and they had to abide by the company policies or contractors had to take what they could get. When times are good and world markets are up, the supply of professional people is low for the demand and the companies pay out higher rates. The reverse is also true. When the demand is low, the supply is usually low.

The cost of living didn't go down either. For a small population that are generally hard-working industrious Kiwis, we were looking to alternatives to support our families. By mid-2006, a number of us electricians were introduced to the mining and resources boom on the West Island, AUSTRALIA.

The white water rafting expedition Kai Tuna River.
Be careful what you wish for. It might just happen.

In the months to come in early 2006, ten of us under the umbrella of the Salvation Army church planned for a final white water rafting adventure, this time a little closer to home and with the guidance of a friend who had his own white water rafting business based in Rotorua, quite often known as Sulphur City or Roto Vegas. Cam was my friend's name.

Rotorua is about a 45-minute drive from Tauranga directly, although the river and point we intended to launch the raft was about twenty minutes from Tauranga. The river is called the Kai Tuna River. Kai in Maori means food and tuna means fish (FISH FOOD). This river is a very fast-flowing river and downstream is an eight meter water fall drop. At the bottom of the fall is the remnant of an old turbine power station and a water depth of about forty meters. Does that scare you? Not us, we are all adrenaline junkies except for dragging in the minister who had no clue what he was in for. The rest of us were all in for a good time.

Just to confuse us, Cam played a prank on us. He suggested that we take a silver fern (which was one of the national symbols of New Zealand) and throw it in the water. If it lands upside down, you land upside down going over the waterfall. That got the unsuspected thinking. We knew it was a prank.

We were told if we fell out and got sucked down to go into the fetal position. The buoyancy of the water will haul you back up. That was true.

This time round, I had my brother-in-law Peter then Ian, Mark, Trent, Big Dave, the minister Paul and three others. We had two big rafts all kitted out and wet suits, helmets, and life jackets. Paul was the most scared of the lot. The rest of us were hanging out for the big drop. We turned around and paddled against the current at one point to see how strong it was. It was strong. Then we turned around again to go with the flow of the current. We were in front of the raft, paddling, keeping straight and fast-approaching the massive big drop. And it came. Straight over we went, we airborne for just a few seconds and hit the raging current. We all stayed in as the raft hit the river with a big thump. We didn't capsize, WOOHOO, and not one of us fell out. The look on Ian and Big Dave's face. It was classic. A very fun moment. We had been airborne for about thirty seconds and dropped eight meters. The old power station was on the left. From there, we quickly paddled into calmer waters and waited for the others. This would be a sight to see. They came, they were airborne for about thirty seconds, they hit the water and three of them, including Paul, went flying out. We had a WOOHOO and a great laugh. The three all managed to get back in the raft. I think Paul was not shellshocked but raft-shocked. It was so funny.

You had to be there to see it.

A big cheer by all. Most of us are adrenaline junkies, always waiting for the big splash when on the water.

We did paddle downstream a bit further. The actual river is the out flow from Lakes Rotorua and Rotoiti. It flows northwards for 45 kms, emptying into the Bay of Plenty in the TASMAN SEA near the township of Tepuke. We would have paddled about fifteen to twenty kilometers.

If you want to help someone cure their fear of rushing water, take them white water rafting down the Kaituna River. Don't tell them what they are in for.

We had another woman minister a few years ago who was called on to be part of a fundraiser for the Duke of Edinburgh awards scheme for young people going to Japan and Scotland. She was asked whether she could lead the event. Without really thinking about it, she said yes.

She was needed to jump out of a plane at 10000 feet and every 1000 feet, she was sponsored. Lee was petrified of heights but she couldn't back out of the answer she had given. The day she was to make the jump as a tandem dive, she was petrified of getting into the plane. However, she got in and did the jump from 10000 feet. She enjoyed it and overcame her fear of heights, raising money for the sponsorship at the same time.

Going back to white water rafting in New Zealand or any other venture there, you just got to do it. Down the South Island of New Zealand, the rivers that flow from the glacier lakes and from the mountains and around Queenstown can be up to category 5, some up to category 5 in the North Island when the flood gates of hydro dams are open as well.

All in all, we had a great trip and a great day. Paul's face was a classic all that afternoon. I think he hadn't got over the shock. However, he came right for the Sunday as he preached his sermon on the living water.

This won't be the final expedition. We here in Aus are gearing up to do some more outlandish expeditions in the future, both here and New Zealand. Aussies usually team up with Kiwis to have some fun as well...WATCH THIS SPACE. COME AND JOIN US.

We were just a group of fellas, nothing special, who got together and will get together again. I am sure to have some fun and fellowship.

Not long after these events, I became very ill. One Sunday morning, I woke vomiting so badly, I couldn't even get out of bed. Vijaya called the emergency doctor and she suggested I take this prescription from the chemist. I told her that I could not hold anything down and would only vomit it back up. So she asked me to come in right away.

The doctor looked at me and right away knew the problem. She asked me, "Does it hurt down on the right side above your hip?"

"Yes," I replied.

"You got to go to the hospital right away. You have appendicitis."

I was rushed to the hospital right away by my wife. The hospital knew I was coming. The nurse placed me on a trolley, and I was taken for scans and checks and was placed for emergency surgery early the next day. My wife was holding my hand all the way. She came back early in the morning just before I was anesthetised. I had the operation early that morning. The doctors told me my appendix had nearly burst and the situation could have been extremely dangerous. However, I was pumped on a drip full of antibiotics. For the next three days, I could not go to the toilet. But when I eventually did go, both ends never stopped flowing. Not too good for the person coming in behind. I was in the hospital for about four days, realizing how such a small operation, which could have been a serious outcome, had taken so much out of me.

> *Do not take life too seriously. You will never get out alive.*
> — ALBERT HUBBARD —

When I think back to my journeys through life this far, I am amazed at the awesomeness of the universe. There's a creator with his own hand who put every detail of the universe together and breathed life into it. And if we are made in his image, he must have a good sense of humor.

When we can laugh at ourselves and make others laugh, it brings down barriers. It is a pathway for enjoying other people's company. Laughter creates intimacy and it unites.

There are times we have to be serious when making important decisions but to reduce stress and anxiety, don't dwell on problems which seem to worry a lot of young people today. The world puts so much pressure on young people, on how they should conform, how they should look, and what the future holds for them. Many see only doom and gloom.

My predecessors always told me to look for the best in people, in courage people, don't take life to seriously, plan always, have plan B. Never let anyone tell you that you cannot achieve what you have been created to be. Never limit yourself, take a risk, if you fail get up again and try a different approach. People are always admired when the determination and commitment to achieving a goal is realised. Before leaving New Zealand for the mines of Australia, I did my last flight in a light twin engine piper Aztec, taking a charter out to White Island, THE VOLCANIC ISLAND, and to a power station not far from Tauranga. It wouldn't be till a few years later in Australia that again I would be flying in a light twin engine aircraft.

I still hold New Zealand and Commercial Pilot licenses.

Also in recent years, I was able to get my turbine rating endorsed on an agricultural aircraft, the Fletcher Cresco. This is a jet turbine aircraft with a propeller not a jet turbo fan. Also this aircraft could take off with a load within very short distances and land with power on breaking or meaning reversing the pitch of the propeller blade, therefore it lands very short.

Being endorsed to fly a Cessna 206 on floats was also very interesting, as it was a boat on water with rudders on the pods and,

when airborne, was a plane.

I flew on and off the Lake Taupo, landing on the rivers that feed into Lake Taupo. One of these rivers had a power station at the end and I had to be careful when taking off.

Also we were able to have some fun with some water skiing on the lake with the seaplane.

Before leaving to work in the North West Queensland Isa mines, Vijaya and I thought would be a good idea to take Rachel and Cilla to the Gold Coast for eight days.

We had an apartment in Surfers Paradise just near the beach. We spent some time there and also went to the theme parks, Dream World and Water World and a few others.

Everything was going all right till I got on this ride called the CLAW. Now I have done spins, loops, barrel rolls, and spins in an aerobatic aircraft but this thing ruined my day. It worked three dimensions, arms going out up and down the cab. We were harnessed in. We spun and then the thing turning clockwise and the floor dropped out. When I got off this contraption, I had to go to the sick bay for about three hours. I was still going up and down, my head was spinning, and I couldn't even walk straight. I did come right and the rest of the time spent at the Gold Coast was great.

> *The difference between stupidity and genius*
> *is that genius has its limits.*
> — ALBERT EINSTEIN —

Within a month of coming back from the Gold Coast, I was leaving with a few other electricians. I left to join the mining boom at Mt Isa Mines in North Queensland. My good friend Ronald and Jemma from Tauranga had worked there years before. It was a mining town with all the facilities. All of us were accommodated at the Irish Club mining accommodation.

When flying into Mt Isa from Brisbane, my first impression was that I've landed in the middle of the desert and in this desert is a town with a big mine on the other side of the railway tracks. We had been contracted to Downer EDI Mt Isa for a project underground. At that time, Mt Isa mines was owned by a Swedish company called Xstrata. Xstrata had been upgrading some of their underground ore carrying conveyor systems. We were part of the electrical team that were called to do this upgrade.

My first reaction was that I'm not going underground and the manager said, "We need you down there." In the end, I did. We had to do both the surface inductions for Mt Isa mines as every area of Mt Isa Mines from the copper smelter to the lead concentrator, site services, the power station, hoisting and underground have all their own training programs initially for safety.

So we had a full four days of surface and underground training. The underground training was quite specific as you had your battery pack which had a pager with it, a self-rescuer, a respirator, and also a cap lap with a cord attached to the battery pack. We were briefed about the gases that could arise at times called STENCH GASES; they smell like rotten eggs. We were briefed about our self-rescue packs and how to wear them in an emergency. We were shown where the emergency rescue chambers were on each level underground and what was in them and how long the oxygen would last for. We were even trained to do scaling, which is using a long bar with a flat end to chafe off any loose rock or report any possible rock falls.

Mt Isa mines has well over thirty levels and over the years we have only been down as far as thirty, which is where the ore crusher is. The blasting is down around the thirty-fifth level or more at 8.00 am and 8.00 pm. By the way, the whole town rocks depending where they are blasting.

We were working on twenty-two and our crib room was up on the eighteenth level. Driving down there, you had to be passed out or trained to drive all those levels, as there are some levels not used anymore and the unfamiliar person could get lost. When driving sometimes you had to go down to come back up and there is about five to ten kilometres off-roading down there.

We were on level twenty-two as I said and were upgrading all the control systems. Program or PLC boards were changing over from lead to copper or might have been the other way around. So there were local control station boxes for motors on the conveyor drive side and motor change outs as well. I was working in the small room terminating and connecting the PLC input and output connections. This is in July, the winter months in Queensland, and it was extremely hot down there. We were working a night shift, day or night doesn't matter down there, conditions are still the same. Before we could start on our shift, we had to electronically tag in and be in our safe working area when they were going to do the blasting at 8.00 pm. If you are tagged in that time in the blasting area, they would ask questions and that person needs to be found as they hold up production and yes, you could lose your job for that too. Most of the working areas had ram air blasted through ducting by huge fans and areas that were pressurised for steel door closures.

Some of these doors were prior to entering operator's cabs or workshops.

This night we had tagged on for the safe blasting area and drove down to our crib room, which was our safe blasting area. That night I was lying down on the bench seat not feeling too well. The fellas looked at me and, seeing me white as a sheet, insisted I needed to be taken to the hospital after blasting complete had been registered on our pagers.

I was driven up to the surface and taken to the accident and emergency. Entering the front door and going towards the nurses' station, I threw up all over the floor. A doctor came out and immediately knew I was completely dehydrated. I sweat profusely in the heat and not being acclimatised, I was drinking a lot of iced water, which was going straight out of me. Dehydration can be dangerous as it can cause your body to overheat so badly, it can shut down your organs.

The nurse put an IV drip in my arm to rehydrate me. They asked me a few questions to make sure I knew where I was. The doctor came and told me that electrolytes were required in small doses to keep the salt in my body.

I rang my sister Marie and told her where I was and what had happened. I didn't want to worry my wife as she to this day dislikes me working underground.

That night, there was a major incident happened with the fellas. After dropping me off, my colleagues went back down to level 22, working through the night. A few levels up, a TA had been throwing scrap steel into a skip bin on the cage. The cage is what carries persons, vehicles and equipment down the shaft. Well, this bit of steel missed the bin and came right down the shaft. One of my colleagues had just walked away to get something for where he was working and the dropped steel landed where he was working. If it had been there any longer, he would have been impaled.

These fellows drove back up to the surface a little shaken. The level above and below were closed off and there was a big safety investigation. Everything had to be left as it was so every aspect of the cause was looked at and to prevent another situation occurring. Unfortunately, I have seen this happen again in later years on the maintenance side of the cage, this time from the surface all the way down the shaft.

This was just the introduction to my mining career. We spent five weeks working twelve-hour nights as you do on these sites to get the project close to finished. It was a five-week on, two-week off project so at the end of five weeks, I was flown back to New Zealand and came back after my break for a new project on the surface. This was a new ball and sag mill for the number two lead concentrator. These big mills crush up the ore even further into fine dust with big steel balls in the ball mill. There is a process after that where the copper is extracted through ponds and agitators.

So we were cabling and running and terminating all the PLC cables into the cabinets, so the engineers could test and make the programs up for the mills. The monitors in the control room detail every aspect of pressure, water flow, opening and closing of valves through solenoids, and the VSD (variable speed drives) to the on and off position of some very big electric motors. There were another couple of incidents on this job but I will leave that for another time.

We spent another three to four swings on this project to see it up and running. Four weeks on, seven days off. It was two days of travel either side back to New Zealand.

> *Good advice is something a man gives*
> *when he is too old to set a bad example.*
> — FRANCOIS DELA ROCHEFOUCAULD —

I was back in New Zealand just before Christmas that year and I stayed another six months in Tauranga, coming back to Australia mining in late 2007. In that six months, I was in New Zealand finishing off all my flying contracts with Burns Aviation and working with a friend who had a communications company. I was just the technician installing all his fixed power supplies for running his telecommunication stations. This would be in business center's and remote repeater station on VHF radio.

These were the preceding months before the global financial crisis and I had this section to build a new house that just sitting vacant. My friend Ronald had a building contractor partnership with a registered builder who was keen to start a building contract on this section with my designed house plans.

Not knowing what was coming globally in the next year, I proceeded to take a mortgage out with the bank to build this house. I had saved a lot of money from the mining projects in the last twelve months and put this into the house projects as well. The section was 800 square meters, a really large section, and the house was brick and tile, four bedrooms with open kitchen dining, lounge, two bathrooms, office, double garage, nice backyard. It had been prewired by an electrical contractor and I had finished the electrical when I came back from Australia.

In this time back in New Zealand, I made one last trip in Ronald's Piper Cherokee 140 light aircraft to drop one of my daughters in Matamata with my mother for the day and then fly with my father down the center of the North Island, across Lake Taupo, across the desert road where the military play their war games, through military airspace with permission, then into Palmerston North to pick up my other daughter Cilla.

The Desert Road runs through the Tongariro National Park, which is 3536 feet above sea level. So my altimeter was set to sea level barometric pressure and I was flying at an altitude of 8000 feet, over the Desert Rd. We were actually only 4464 feet above the ground level and you could see all the military tank tracks from that height and their firing ranges. Fortunately it was not active. First I would not have been allowed to fly through there and secondly it is not a good day when accidental ammunition comes flying through the cockpit.

We landed in Palmerston North within two hours. I picked up my daughter, and we flew back the way we came. All clear on the military front and back across the great bottomless Lake Taupo. We had left Matamata at 1000 hours and were back by 1500 hours. One half hour stop in Palmerston North.

If we had driven this trip, it would have taken five hours either way. So I dropped Dad off in Matamata, picked up Rachel and had Cilla with me. I was back in Tauranga by 1600 hours. It was clear skies that day as well.

> *Don't worry about the world coming to an end today,*
> *it is already tomorrow in Australia.*
> — CHARLES M. SHULTZ —

Our new house was being built whilst I was away working from June 2007 that year in Queensland, Australia.

Downer Engineering had asked me to go back to Mt Isa to work at the Stanwell power station. This was for maintenance and running capacity of power station working with the existing staff. During that time I had spent ten weeks away from home and decided to bring my two girls with my mother to the Isa for a twelve-day outback experience. You either like Mt Isa or you get out of there as quick as you can. I didn't mind it for the times I have worked there. There is a bit of history there as the township, or should I say the city of Mt Isa, is built around the mine. The mine itself has been in existence since the 1920s and there is a wealth of minerals in this area. So they came, Mum and my two girls who were still at high school on their holiday break. They flew out from Auckland, New Zealand to Mt Isa via Brisbane. I had booked a motel for them, hired a rental car, drove around the area. Showed them Lake Moondara, which supplies the water for Mt Isa and the mine, the underground hospital built during the Second World War as a precaution against a Japanese invasion. I even went on an underground mining tour with them dressed up in all the mining equipment. Yes, my mother came as well. She was 73 years younger then. Rachel and Cilla were able to go swimming, they even came to the Irish club restaurant for meals where I was staying.

In between working, I would stay the night at the motel and walk to catch the bus to the site in the morning. I spent as much time as I could with Rachel, Cilla and Mum. They really appreciated that. I know Mum did as it would be her last trip out of New Zealand she would make due to health issues she had to deal with later.

The day they were leaving, one of my Maori friends drove them to the airport. Yes, Australia is full of Kiwis and we help Aussies do the work.

Saying goodbye to your family, either going to work from New Zealand or seeing them leave you from where you are, is very hard. I remember leaving early in the mornings, catching the shuttle bus to Auckland for a flight across the Tasman, working in the mines and saying goodbye to my daughters and wife. Cilla would hold on to me and say, "Daddy, don't go," and my reply was, "I have to go to work." It's not a nice feeling, I can tell you that.

Eventually my family did come to Australia and live in Townsville.

Having landed at Brisbane Airport one day coming from New Zealand, I transferred to the domestic terminal. Three silly people had breached security and literally the whole of the airport passengers had to come back and go through security again. There were huge queues and all domestic flights were delayed. So I didn't arrive back at Mt Isa till late that night.

My house was being built and we would be moving in March 2008. We were only months away from the Global Financial Crisis and we had borrowed at a high interest rate on the housing market. I had kept working across the Tasman as this was the only way I saw being able to pay down on my loans quickly. The Kiwi dollar was lower than the Aussie dollar at the time by about eighteen cents and earnings were greater. You could actually save from what you earned. My working accommodation was free and all my meals were included in my accommodation. All that was required of us was you follow the rules and go to work.

Right up until June 2008, everything was going great. I was flying in the outback on my new Australian commercial license. We even had an Air-force F18 playing with us in the air one day. It was a lone American F18 flying in and around us. His call sign was HAWK as we picked up his radio transmission. At first I thought of all the aircraft I knew, Sky Hawk, Black Hawk, Tomma Hawk before I realised it was an F18. He came screaming in behind us at Mt Isa airport. The engineer in the back seat quickly opened the door whilst we were taxiing on the runway, filmed the F18 front on.

He did take off again not long after, went vertical, and disappeared out of sight.

The engineers who I had been working with had even planned a weekend flight to Boulia, a small township 186 km south of Mt Isa. This is where they have the annual camel races. It was that Friday night that everything came to a halt globally. The share market and the banking systems from the USA had collapsed, sending a rippling effect around the world.

Projects were stopped. We were given the ultimatum to stay and work if there was work, otherwise Downer Engineering would fly us home the next day. Literally the mining companies just stopped all their projects and only their maintenance was carried forward.

My family was back in New Zealand and I couldn't stay. Because of that decision, I was gone. For three months, I lived off my Australian tax return. There was no work in New Zealand. We had just built a house, the bottom had literally fallen out of the housing market, I was still paying high interest on the loan and my savings would be reduced to shreds. We had set up a family trust with Vijaya, myself, and a friend on that trust. We weren't sure what we were going to do but we weren't going to let it beat us.

The fellas that stayed on in Australia told me their work situation was intermittent. Very unsure times. It was tough. WHEN THE GOING GETS TOUGH, THE TOUGH GET GOING. Yes, for a while, I was really living on nothing. There would be times again I would face these challenges. But you know what? I am grateful because God gives me the resources not to live on security but to take action. My dream now is to build a business with a system. This idea would be shown to me in years to come.

I did come back to Australia, bought a small apartment, and brought my family over at the beginning of 2010. We have had our challenges. We rented our house out in New Zealand for a time and then the bank wanted it more than we did. We missed that house but we had to move on.

Cilla, my youngest daughter, finished her schooling here in Townsville and she has moved on in recent years to Melbourne. Rachel went back to New Zealand for three years and eventually came back and is working towards her studies and traveling.

Life hasn't always been easy for Vijaya as she has lived in three different countries and I know she misses her extended family, although she has had the opportunity to go and see them many times.

For myself I still continue to venture forward. I have seen so many opportunities arise here in Australia. I will later write another book on all the experiences and dangers I have gone through in this land.

But as I finish this part of my journey in this story, I am thankful to friends and family around the world and, more importantly, thankful to a loving God. THE LORD IS MY SHEPARD I SHALL NOT WANT, the beginning of the Psalm.

EPILOGUE

Before you judge a man, walk a mile in his shoes.
After that who cares. He's a mile away and you've got his shoes.
— BILLY CONNOLLY —

He who laughs last gets the joke.
— CHARLES DE GAULLE —

If you are going to tell the truth,
be funny or they will kill you.
— BILLY WILD —

We never really grow up, we only learn how to act in public.
— BRYAN WHITE —

If you think you are too small to make a difference,
try sleeping with a mosquito.
— DALAI LAMA —

Never under any circumstances take a sleeping pill
and a laxative on the same night.
— DAVE BARRY —

Try laughing more often. It's contagious, it attracts and it reduces stress. Circumstances bring out quotes from these people above. Not sure about Billy Connolly, as he is character in himself.

But the point I am making is that not everything goes to plan in life but if we can see the funny side and surround ourselves with happy people, our outlook on life is a lot better.

Not so long ago, I was flying back from a mine site in Western Australia. My friend who I call my booking agent had been out fighting fires with the rural fire department. He had booked me on a flight from Perth to Townsville. Being very tired that night, he had booked the ticket without realizing it was booked a month in advance. I had flown in, checking my bags with Qantas check in. The woman laughing said, "Mr Stewart, the ticket has been booked a month in advance." To upgrade it was going cost quite a bit more for that flight as the flight was full. So I decided to travel the next day. I made arrangements to be driven to this Qantas accommodation, thinking he had booked this except he had booked me somewhere else. I was picked up by accommodation transport. I went to check in and there was no record. Having phoned my friend who had booked me somewhere else, I could not get this business to drop me at the oppositions accommodation free of charge, so decided to stay there. I did get some sleep and home the next day.

There are lots of funny things in my mining travel log I will write in my next book. BUT DON'T TAKE LIFE TOO SERIOUSLY.

I pay tribute to my Mum, Dad, and to all my siblings, and my good friend Frank who encouraged to write this book.

Also I want to pay tribute to extended family and friends who have had a positive input in my life growing up and who have even mentored me over the years. If it was not for these gracious people, things could have a little different in my life's journey.

HONOR
A man's pride shall bring him low,
but honor shall uphold the humble in spirit.
— PROVERBS 29:3 —

I have my health, I have my sanity, I have my family and many great events and new people to meet in the future. We may all go through crisis but how we deal with them is up to us. The human spirit is a wonderful thing. It can be built up by those around us or can be crushed with a few short words. I choose to build up people who are willing to learn and learn from their mistakes as I have done and may make in the future.

And I choose to love the unloved as well.

Put God first in everything you do.
Everything I have is by the grace of God. It's a gift.
I didn't always stick with Him but He stuck with me.
— DENZEL WASHINGTON —

This is my story as well...Richard J. Stewart

PHOTO DESCRIPTIONS
PLUS ADDITIONAL PHOTOS

Page 1, top	My mum, Brenda Armitage, in her early 20's was a nurse in Yorkshire UK
Page 1, bottom	International Scout Jamboree in England. New Zealand contingent, 1957.
Page 3	My English maternal grandparents Arthur and Phyllis Armitage, and my grandmother's mother and sibling.
Page 4	My father, Robert James Campbell Stewart, my brother, Andrew David Stewart, and myself.
Page 5	Myself receiving the Duke of Edinburgh Gold award from the Governor General Sir Keith Holyoak in November, 1979
Page 6	My mum, Brenda Stewart
Page 7, top	My New Zealand paternal grandfather Willy Stewart's military unit, 1943.
Page 7, bottom	Dad's scout troop on tour in Australia doing a presentation, 1957.
Page 19	Myself in a small town called Delft in the Netherlands.
Page 22	Museum/Hotel in Arnheim in the Netherlands near the location of one of the last major battles of WW2
Page 23, top	Arnhem Cemetery
Page 23, bottom	Various displays from the museum
Page 26	Hitchhiking through Switzerland
Page 39	A Royal Canadian mounted policemen in dress uniform
Page 54	My friend, Daniel and I, in uniform
Page 56	My friend, Daniel
Page 66	Wellington South Salvation Army band on tour in Australia
Page 70, top	Wellington South Salvation Army band at the Brisbane Temple Salvation Army Church
Page 70, bottom	Wellington South Salvation Army band visiting a school and playing for them in Maryborough Australia
Page 75	Flying into Wellington Airport New Zealand
Page 80	My sister, Fiona
Page 90	My Dad, Robert James Campbell Stewart
Page 102	Drawing of Mum by Dad while he was in Lurigancho Prison
Page 103	My Dad writing
Page 124	My daughters, Rachel and Cilla in Gisborne New Zealand
Page 151	On Lake Taupo, New Zealand

— ADDITIONAL PHOTOS ON THE NEXT PAGES —

Gisborne New Zealand Port and Beaches

Gisborne New Zealand Beach

Interesting fact: In early 1945, a German U boat sailed into the Port of Gisborne under darkness looking for cargo ships sailing to England with needed food and supplies to blow up. It had already torpedoed ships off Australia's eastern seaboard. It was a Saturday night and the crew saw no ships and a Saturday night dancing. The sub quietly sailed out and moved down the east coast of both islands and was eventually recalled to Malaysia where it was based under the Axis Treaty between Germany and Japan till the war ended in Europe May 8th, 1945.

Sunrise in Townsville

My beautiful family - wife, Vijaya, and daughters, Rachel and Cilla

www.ingramcontent.com/pod-product-compliance
Lightning Source LLC
LaVergne TN
LVHW091549060526
838200LV00036B/760